Ariel

THE RESTORED EDITION

*A facsimile of Plath's manuscript,
reinstating her original selection
and arrangement*

Sylvia Plath

Foreword by Frieda Hughes

ff

faber and faber

Ariel first published in 1965
by Faber and Faber Limited
3 Queen Square, London WC1N 3AU

Ariel: The Restored Edition first published in Great Britain in 2004
by Faber and Faber Limited
3 Queen Square, London WC1N 3AU
and in the United States by HarperCollins Publishers

Printed in England by T. J. International Ltd, Padstow, Cornwall

The facsimiles found here are reproductions of the originals from the
Sylvia Plath Collection, Mortimer Rare Book Room, Smith College.

Grateful acknowledgment to Karen Kukil, Associate Curator,
Mortimer Rare Book Room, Smith College.

An extension of this copyright page, and the previous publishing history of
the Plath works collected here, appears in the Notes section,
beginning on page 195.

A CIP record for this book
is available from the British Library
ISBN 0–571–22685–X

2 4 6 8 10 9 7 5 3 1

Ariel

THE RESTORED EDITION

Other Books by Sylvia Plath

Contents

Foreword

This edition of *Ariel* by my mother, Sylvia Plath, exactly follows the arrangement of her last manuscript as she left it. As her daughter I can only approach it, and its divergence from the first United Kingdom publication of *Ariel* in 1965 and subsequent United States publication in 1966, both edited by my father, Ted Hughes, from the purely personal perspective of its history within my family.

When she committed suicide on February 11, 1963, my mother left a black spring binder on her desk, containing a manuscript of forty poems. She probably last worked on the manuscript's arrangement in mid-November 1962. 'Death & Co.', written on the fourteenth of that month is the last poem to be included in her list of contents. She wrote an additional nineteen poems before her death, six of which she finished before our move to London from Devon on December 12, and a further thirteen in the last eight weeks of her life. These poems were left on her desk with the manuscript.

The first cleanly typed page of the manuscript gives the title of the collection as *Ariel and other poems*. On the two sheets that follow, alternative titles had been tried out, each title scored out in turn and a replacement handwritten above it. On one sheet the title was altered from *The Rival* to *A Birthday Present* to *Daddy*. On the other, the title changed from *The Rival* to *The Rabbit Catcher* to *A Birthday Present* to *Daddy*. These new title poems are in chronological order (July 1961, May 1962, September 1962, and October 1962) and give an idea of earlier possible dates of her rearrangement of the working manuscript.

When *Ariel* was first published, edited by my father, it was a somewhat different collection from the manuscript my mother left behind. My father had roughly followed the order of my mother's contents list, taking twelve poems out of the U.S. publication, and thirteen out of the U.K. publication. He replaced these with ten selected for the U.K. edition, and twelve selected for the U.S. edition. These he chose from the nineteen very late poems written after mid-November 1962, and three earlier poems.

There was no lack of choice. Since the publication of *The Colossus* in 1960, my mother had written many poems that showed an advance on her earlier work. These were transitional poems between the very different styles of *The Colossus* and *Ariel* (a selection of them was published in *Crossing the Water* in 1971). But towards the end of 1961, poems in the *Ariel* voice began to appear here and there among the transitional poems. They had an urgency, freedom, and force that was quite new in her work. In October 1961, there was 'The Moon and the Yew Tree' and 'Little Fugue'; 'An Appearance' followed in April 1962. From this point, all the poems she wrote were in the distinctive *Ariel* voice. They are poems of an otherworldly, menacing landscape:

> This is the light of the mind, cold and planetary.
> The trees of the mind are black. The light is blue.
> The grasses unload their griefs on my feet as if I were God,
> . . . .
> I simply cannot see where there is to get to.
> ('The Moon and the Yew Tree')

Then, still in early April 1962, she wrote 'Among the Narcissi' and 'Pheasant', moments of perfect poetic poise, tranquil and melancholy— the calm before the storm:

> You said you would kill it this morning.
> Do not kill it. It startles me still,
> The jut of the odd, dark head, pacing
>
> Through the uncut grass on the elm's hill.
> ('Pheasant')

After that, the poems came with increasing frequency, ease, and ferocity, culminating in October 1962 when she wrote twenty-five major poems. Her very last poems were written six days before she died. In all, she left around seventy poems in the unique *Ariel* voice.

On work-connected visits to London in June 1962, my father began an affair with a woman who had incurred my mother's jealousy a month earlier. My mother, somehow learning of the affair, was enraged. In July her mother, Aurelia, came to stay at Court Green, our thatched black and white cob house in Devon, for a long visit. Tensions increased between my parents, my mother proposing separation, though they travelled to Galway together that September to find a house where my mother could stay for the winter. By early October, with encouragement from Aurelia (whose efforts I witnessed as a small child), my mother ordered my father out of the house.

My father went up to London where he first stayed with friends, and then around Christmas rented a flat in Soho. He told me many years later that, despite her apparent determination, he thought my mother might reconsider. 'We were working towards it when she died,' he said.

Deciding against the house in Galway, my mother moved my brother and me to London in December 1962, to the flat she had rented in what was once Yeats's house in Fitzroy Road. Until her death, my father visited us there almost daily, often babysitting when my mother needed time for herself.

Although my mother was in London for eight weeks before she died, my father had left her with their house in Devon, the joint bank account, the black Morris Traveller (their car), and was giving her money to support us. When my mother died, my father had insufficient funds to cover the funeral, and my grandfather, William Hughes, paid for it.

My father eventually returned to Devon with my brother and me in September 1963, when his sister, Olwyn, came over from Paris to help take care of us. She stayed with us for two years. My father continued to see 'the other woman' on visits to London, but she remained living primarily with her husband for two and a half years after my mother's death.

Throughout their time together my mother had shown her poems to my father as she wrote them. But after May 1962, when their serious differences began, she kept the poems to herself. My father read 'Event' in the *Observer* that winter and was dismayed to see their private business made the subject of a poem.

My mother had described her *Ariel* manuscript as beginning with the word 'Love' and ending with the word 'Spring', and it was clearly geared to cover the ground from just before the breakup of the marriage to the resolution of a new life, with all the agonies and furies in between. The breakdown of the marriage had defined all my mother's other pain and given it direction. It brought a theme to the poetry. But the *Ariel* voice was there already in the poems of late 1961 and early 1962. It was as though it had been waiting, practising itself, and had found a subject on which it could really get a grip. The manuscript was digging up everything that must be shed in order to move on. 'Berck-Plage', for instance, written in June 1962, is about the funeral that month of a neighbour, Percy Key, but it is also tangled with the grievous loss of her father, Otto, when she was a child. My parents became beekeepers that summer, like Otto, who had been an expert on bees, and his presence stalks the five bee poems in the U.S. version of *Ariel* (four in the U.K. edition).

In December 1962, my mother was asked by BBC radio to read some of her poems for a broadcast, and for this she wrote her own introductions. Her commentaries were dry and brief and she makes no mention of herself as a character in the poems. She might expose herself, but she did not need to point it out. I particularly like two of them: 'In this next poem, the speaker's horse is proceeding at a slow, cold walk down a hill of macadam to the stable at the bottom. It is December. It is foggy. In the fog there are sheep.' ('Sheep in Fog', though one of the poems she included in her broadcast with the *Ariel* poems, was not listed on my mother's contents page in the manuscript—it was only finished in January 1963. My father included it in the first published version of *Ariel*.) For the title poem my mother simply writes: 'Another horseback riding poem, this one called 'Ariel', after a horse I'm especially fond of.'

These introductions made me smile; they have to be the most understated commentaries imaginable for poems that are pared down to their sharpest points of imagery and delivered with tremendous skill. When I read them I imagine my mother, reluctant to undermine with explanation the concentrated energy she'd poured into her verse, in order to preserve its ability to shock and surprise.

In considering *Ariel* for publication my father had faced a dilemma. He was well aware of the extreme ferocity with which some of my mother's poems dismembered those close to her—her husband, her mother, her father, and my father's uncle Walter, even neighbours and acquaintances. He wished to give the book a broader perspective in order to make it more acceptable to readers, rather than alienate them. He felt that some of the nineteen late poems, written after the manuscript was completed, should be represented. 'I simply wanted to make it the best book I could,' he told me. He was aware that many of my mother's new poems had been turned down by magazines because of their extreme nature, though editors still in possession of her poems published them quickly when she died.

My father left out some of the more lacerating poems. 'Lesbos', for instance, though published in the U.S. version of *Ariel,* was taken out of the British edition, as the couple so wickedly depicted in it lived in Cornwall and would have been much offended by its publication. 'Stopped Dead', referring to my father's uncle Walter, was dropped. Some he might otherwise have taken out had been published in period-icals and were already well known. Other omissions—'Magi' and 'Bar-ren Woman', for instance, both from the transitional poems—he simply considered weaker than their replacements. One of the five bee poems, 'The Swarm', was originally included in my mother's contents list, but with brackets around it, and the poem itself was not included in her manuscript of forty poems. My father reinstated it in the U.S. edition.

The poems of the original manuscript my father left out were: 'The Rabbit Catcher', 'Thalidomide', 'Barren Woman', 'A Secret', 'The Jailor', 'The Detective', 'Magi', 'The Other', 'Stopped Dead', 'The Courage of Shutting-Up', 'Purdah', 'Amnesiac'. (Though included in the 1966 U.S. version, 'Lesbos' was kept out of the 1965 U.K. edition.)

The poems he put into the edited manuscript for publication were: 'The Swarm' and 'Mary's Song' (only in the U.S. edition), 'Sheep in Fog', 'The Hanging Man', 'Little Fugue', 'Years', 'The Munich Man-nequins', 'Totem', 'Paralytic', 'Balloons', 'Poppies in July', 'Kindness',

'Contusion', 'Edge', and 'Words'. 'The Swarm' was included in the original contents list, but not in the manuscript.

In 1981 my father published my mother's *Collected Poems* and included in the Notes the contents list of her *Ariel* manuscript. This inclusion brought my father's arrangement under public scrutiny, and he was much criticized for not publishing *Ariel* as my mother had left it, though the extracted poems were included in the *Collected Poems* for all to see.

My father had a profound respect for my mother's work in spite of being one of the subjects of its fury. For him the work was *the* thing, and he saw the care of it as a means of tribute and a responsibility.

But the point of anguish at which my mother killed herself was taken over by strangers, possessed and reshaped by them. The collection of *Ariel* poems became symbolic to me of this possession of my mother and of the wider vilification of my father. It was as if the clay from her poetic energy was taken up and versions of my mother made out of it, invented to reflect only the inventors, as if they could possess my real, actual mother, now a woman who had ceased to resemble herself in those other minds. I saw poems such as 'Lady Lazarus' and 'Daddy' dissected over and over, the moment that my mother wrote them being applied to her whole life, to her whole person, as if they were the total sum of her experience.

Criticism of my father was even levelled at his ownership of my mother's copyright, which fell to him on her death and which he used to directly benefit my brother and me. Through the legacy of her poetry my mother still cared for us, and it was strange to me that anyone would wish it otherwise.

After my mother's suicide and the publication of *Ariel,* many cruel things were written about my father that bore no resemblance to the man who quietly and lovingly (if a little strictly and being sometimes fallible) brought me up—later with the help of my stepmother. All the time, he kept alive the memory of the mother who had left me, so I felt as if she were watching over me, a constant presence in my life.

It appeared to me that my father's editing of *Ariel* was seen to 'interfere' with the sanctity of my mother's suicide, as if, like some deity, everything associated with her must be enshrined and preserved as miraculous. For me, as her daughter, everything associated with her *was* miraculous, but that was because my father made it appear so, even playing me a record of my mother reading her poetry so I could hear her voice again. It was many years before I discovered my mother had a ferocious temper and a jealous streak, in contrast to my father's more temperate and optimistic nature, and that she had on two occasions destroyed my father's work, once by ripping it up and once by burning it. I'd been aghast that my perfect image of her, attached to my last memories, was so unbalanced. But my mother, inasmuch as she was an exceptional poet, was also a human being and I found comfort in restoring the balance; it made sense of her for me. The outbursts were the exception, not the rule. Life at home was generally quiet, and my parents' relationship was hardworking and companionable. However, as her daughter, I needed to know the truth of my mother's nature—as I did my father's—since it was to help me understand my own.

But if I had ever been in doubt that my mother's suicide, rather than her life, was really the reason for her elevation to the feminist icon she became, or whether *Ariel*'s notoriety came from being the manuscript on her desk *when she died,* rather than simply being an extraordinary manuscript, my doubts were dispelled when my mother was accorded a blue plaque in 2000, to be placed on her home in London. Blue plaques are issued by English Heritage to celebrate the contribution of a person's work to the lives of others—and to celebrate their life in the place where they did the living. It was initially proposed that the plaque should be placed on the wall of the property in Fitzroy Road where my mother committed suicide, and I was asked if I would unveil it once it was in place. English Heritage had been led to believe that my mother had done all her best work at that address, when in fact she'd been there for only eight weeks, written thirteen poems, nursed two sick children, been ill herself, furnished and decorated the flat, and killed herself.

So instead, the plaque was put on the wall of 3 Chalcot Square, where my mother and father had their first London home, where they had lived for twenty-one months, where my mother wrote *The Bell Jar,* published *The Colossus*, and gave birth to me. This was a place where she had truly lived and where she'd been happy and productive—with my father. But there was outrage in the national press in England at this—I was even accosted in the street on the day of the unveiling by a man who insisted the plaque was in the wrong place. 'The plaque should be on Fitzroy Road!' he cried, and the newspapers echoed him. I asked one of the journalists why. 'Because,' they replied, 'that was where your mother wrote all her best work.' I explained she'd only been there eight weeks. 'Well, then,' they said, '. . . it's where she was a single mother.' I told them I was unaware that English Heritage gave out blue plaques for single motherhood. Finally they confessed. 'It's because that's where she died.'

'We already have a gravestone,' I replied. 'We don't need another.'

I did not want my mother's death to be commemorated as if it had won an award. I wanted her *life* to be celebrated, the fact that she had existed, lived to the fullness of her ability, been happy and sad, tormented and ecstatic, and given birth to my brother and me. I think my mother was extraordinary in her work, and valiant in her efforts to fight the depression that dogged her throughout her life. She used every emotional experience as if it were a scrap of material that could be pieced together to make a wonderful dress; she wasted nothing of what she felt, and when in control of those tumultuous feelings she was able to focus and direct her incredible poetic energy to great effect. And here was *Ariel*, her extraordinary achievement, poised as she was between her volatile emotional state and the edge of the precipice. The art was not to fall.

Representing my mother's vision and experience at a particular time in her life during great emotional turmoil, these *Ariel* poems—this harnessing of her own inner forces by my mother herself—speak for themselves.

My mother's poems cannot be crammed into the mouths of actors in any filmic reinvention of her story in the expectation that they can breathe life into her again, any more than literary fictionalization of my mother's life—as if writing straight fiction would not get the writer enough notice (or any notice at all)—achieves any purpose other than to parody the life she actually lived. Since she died my mother has been dissected, analyzed, reinterpreted, reinvented, fictionalized, and in some cases completely fabricated. It comes down to this: her own words describe her best, her ever-changing moods defining the way she viewed her world and the manner in which she pinned down her subjects with a merciless eye.

Each poem is put into perspective by the knowledge that in time, the life and observations the poems were written about would have changed, evolved, and moved on as my mother would have done. They build upon all the other writings over the years in my mother's life, and best demonstrate the many complex layers of her inner being.

When she died leaving *Ariel* as her last book, she was caught in the act of revenge, in a voice that had been honed and practised for years, latterly with the help of my father. Though he became a victim of it, ultimately he did not shy away from its mastery.

This new, restored edition is my mother in that moment. It is the basis for the published *Ariel,* edited by my father. Each version has its own significance though the two histories are one.

Frieda Hughes

I

Ariel and other poems

For
Frieda and Nicholas

Morning Song

Love set you going like a fat gold watch.
The midwife slapped your footsoles, and your bald cry
Took its place among the elements.

Our voices echo, magnifying your arrival. New statue
In a drafty museum, your nakedness
Shadows our safety. We stand round blankly as walls.

I'm no more your mother
Than the cloud that distils a mirror to reflect its own slow
Effacement at the wind's hand.

All night your moth-breath
Flickers among the flat pink roses. I wake to listen:
A far sea moves in my ear.

One cry, and I stumble from bed, cow-heavy and floral
In my Victorian nightgown.
Your mouth opens clean as a cat's. The window square

Whitens and swallows its dull stars. And now you try
Your handful of notes;
The clear vowels rise like balloons.

The Couriers

The word of a snail on the plate of a leaf?
It is not mine. Do not accept it.

Acetic acid in a sealed tin?
Do not accept it. It is not genuine.

A ring of gold with the sun in it?
Lies. Lies and a grief.

Frost on a leaf, the immaculate
Cauldron, talking and crackling

All to itself on the top of each
Of nine black Alps,

A disturbance in mirrors,
The sea shattering its grey one——

Love, love, my season.

The Rabbit Catcher

It was a place of force——
The wind gagging my mouth with my own blown hair,
Tearing off my voice, and the sea
Blinding me with its lights, the lives of the dead
Unreeling in it, spreading like oil.

I tasted the malignity of the gorse,
Its black spikes,
The extreme unction of its yellow candle-flowers.
They had an efficiency, a great beauty,
And were extravagant, like torture.

There was only one place to get to.
Simmering, perfumed,
The paths narrowed into the hollow.
And the snares almost effaced themselves——
Zeroes, shutting on nothing,

Set close, like birth pangs.
The absence of shrieks
Made a hole in the hot day, a vacancy.
The glassy light was a clear wall,
The thickets quiet.

I felt a still busyness, an intent.
I felt hands round a tea mug, dull, blunt,
Ringing the white china.
How they awaited him, those little deaths!
They waited like sweethearts. They excited him.

And we, too, had a relationship——
Tight wires between us,

Pegs too deep to uproot, and a mind like a ring
Sliding shut on some quick thing,
The constriction killing me also.

Thalidomide

O half moon——

Half-brain, luminosity——
Negro, masked like a white,

Your dark
Amputations crawl and appal——

Spidery, unsafe.
What glove

What leatheriness
Has protected

Me from that shadow——
The indelible buds,

Knuckles at shoulder-blades, the
Faces that

Shove into being, dragging
The lopped

Blood-caul of absences.
All night I carpenter

A space for the thing I am given,
A love

Of two wet eyes and a screech.
White spit

Of indifference!
The dark fruits revolve and fall.

The glass cracks across,
The image

Flees and aborts like dropped mercury.

The Applicant

First, are you our sort of person?
Do you wear
A glass eye, false teeth or a crutch,
A brace or a hook,
Rubber breasts or a rubber crotch,

Stitches to show something's missing? No, no? Then
How can we give you a thing?
Stop crying.
Open your hand.
Empty? Empty. Here is a hand

To fill it and willing
To bring teacups and roll away headaches
And do whatever you tell it.
Will you marry it?
It is guaranteed

To thumb shut your eyes at the end
And dissolve of sorrow.
We make new stock from the salt.
I notice you are stark naked.
How about this suit——

Black and stiff, but not a bad fit.
Will you marry it?
It is waterproof, shatterproof, proof
Against fire and bombs through the roof.
Believe me, they'll bury you in it.

Now your head, excuse me, is empty.
I have the ticket for that.

Come here, sweetie, out of the closet.
Well, what do you think of *that?*
Naked as paper to start

But in twenty-five years she'll be silver,
In fifty, gold.
A living doll, everywhere you look.
It can sew, it can cook,
It can talk, talk, talk.

It works, there is nothing wrong with it.
You have a hole, it's a poultice.
You have an eye, it's an image.
My boy, it's your last resort.
Will you marry it, marry it, marry it.

Barren Woman

Empty, I echo to the least footfall,
Museum without statues, grand with pillars, porticoes, rotundas.
In my courtyard a fountain leaps and sinks back into itself,
Nun-hearted and blind to the world. Marble lilies
Exhale their pallor like scent.

I imagine myself with a great public,
Mother of a white Nike and several bald-eyed Apollos.
Instead, the dead injure me with attentions, and nothing can happen.
The moon lays a hand on my forehead,
Blank-faced and mum as a nurse.

Lady Lazarus

I have done it again.
One year in every ten
I manage it——

A sort of walking miracle, my skin
Bright as a Nazi lampshade,
My right foot

A paperweight,
My face a featureless, fine
Jew linen.

Peel off the napkin
O my enemy.
Do I terrify?——

The nose, the eye pits, the full set of teeth?
The sour breath
Will vanish in a day.

Soon, soon the flesh
The grave cave ate will be
At home on me

And I a smiling woman.
I am only thirty.
And like the cat I have nine times to die.

This is Number Three.
What a trash
To annihilate each decade.

What a million filaments.
The peanut-crunching crowd
Shoves in to see

Them unwrap me hand and foot——
The big strip tease.
Gentlemen, ladies

These are my hands
My knees.
I may be skin and bone,

Nevertheless, I am the same, identical woman.
The first time it happened I was ten.
It was an accident.

The second time I meant
To last it out and not come back at all.
I rocked shut

As a seashell.
They had to call and call
And pick the worms off me like sticky pearls.

Dying
Is an art, like everything else.
I do it exceptionally well.

I do it so it feels like hell.
I do it so it feels real.
I guess you could say I've a call.

It's easy enough to do it in a cell.
It's easy enough to do it and stay put.
It's the theatrical

Comeback in broad day
To the same place, the same face, the same brute
Amused shout:

'A miracle!'
That knocks me out.
There is a charge

For the eyeing of my scars, there is a charge
For the hearing of my heart——
It really goes.

And there is a charge, a very large charge
For a word or a touch
Or a bit of blood

Or a piece of my hair or my clothes.
So, so, Herr Doktor.
So, Herr Enemy.

I am your opus,
I am your valuable,
The pure gold baby

That melts to a shriek.
I turn and burn.
Do not think I underestimate your great concern.

Ash, ash——
You poke and stir.
Flesh, bone, there is nothing there——

A cake of soap,
A wedding ring,
A gold filling.

Herr God, Herr Lucifer
Beware
Beware.

Out of the ash
I rise with my red hair
And I eat men like air.

Tulips

The tulips are too excitable, it is winter here.
Look how white everything is, how quiet, how snowed-in.
I am learning peacefulness, lying by myself quietly
As the light lies on these white walls, this bed, these hands.
I am nobody; I have nothing to do with explosions.
I have given my name and my day-clothes up to the nurses
And my history to the anesthetist and my body to surgeons.

They have propped my head between the pillow and the sheet-cuff
Like an eye between two white lids that will not shut.
Stupid pupil, it has to take everything in.
The nurses pass and pass, they are no trouble,
They pass the way gulls pass inland in their white caps,
Doing things with their hands, one just the same as another,
So it is impossible to tell how many there are.

My body is a pebble to them, they tend it as water
Tends to the pebbles it must run over, smoothing them gently.
They bring me numbness in their bright needles, they bring me sleep.
Now I have lost myself I am sick of baggage——
My patent leather overnight case like a black pillbox,
My husband and child smiling out of the family photo;
Their smiles catch onto my skin, little smiling hooks.

I have let things slip, a thirty-year-old cargo boat
Stubbornly hanging on to my name and address.
They have swabbed me clear of my loving associations.
Scared and bare on the green plastic-pillowed trolley
I watched my teaset, my bureaus of linen, my books
Sink out of sight, and the water went over my head.
I am a nun now, I have never been so pure.

I didn't want any flowers, I only wanted
To lie with my hands turned up and be utterly empty.
How free it is, you have no idea how free——
The peacefulness is so big it dazes you,
And it asks nothing, a name tag, a few trinkets.
It is what the dead close on, finally; I imagine them
Shutting their mouths on it, like a Communion tablet.

The tulips are too red in the first place, they hurt me.
Even through the gift paper I could hear them breathe
Lightly, through their white swaddlings, like an awful baby.
Their redness talks to my wound, it corresponds.
They are subtle: they seem to float, though they weigh me down,
Upsetting me with their sudden tongues and their color,
A dozen red lead sinkers round my neck.

Nobody watched me before, now I am watched.
The tulips turn to me, and the window behind me
Where once a day the light slowly widens and slowly thins,
And I see myself, flat, ridiculous, a cut-paper shadow
Between the eye of the sun and the eyes of the tulips,
And I have no face, I have wanted to efface myself.
The vivid tulips eat my oxygen.

Before they came the air was calm enough,
Coming and going, breath by breath, without any fuss.
Then the tulips filled it up like a loud noise.
Now the air snags and eddies round them the way a river
Snags and eddies round a sunken rust-red engine.
They concentrate my attention, that was happy
Playing and resting without committing itself.

The walls, also, seem to be warming themselves.
The tulips should be behind bars like dangerous animals;
They are opening like the mouth of some great African cat,

And I am aware of my heart: it opens and closes
Its bowl of red blooms out of sheer love of me.
The water I taste is warm and salt, like the sea,
And comes from a country far away as health.

A Secret

A secret! A secret!
How superior.
You are blue and huge, a traffic policeman,
Holding up one palm——

A difference between us?
I have one eye, you have two.
The secret is stamped on you,
Faint, undulant watermark.

Will it show in the black detector?
Will it come out
Wavery, indelible, true
Through the African giraffe in its Edeny greenery,

The Moroccan hippopotamus?
They stare from a square, stiff frill.
They are for export,
One a fool, the other a fool.

A secret! An extra amber
Brandy finger
Roosting and cooing 'You, you'
Behind two eyes in which nothing is reflected but monkeys.

A knife that can be taken out
To pare nails,
To lever the dirt.
'It won't hurt.'

An illegitimate baby——
That big blue head!

How it breathes in the bureau drawer.
'Is that lingerie, pet?

'It smells of salt cod, you had better
Stab a few cloves in an apple,
Make a sachet or
Do away with the bastard.

Do away with it altogether.'
'No, no, it is happy there.'
'But it wants to get out!
Look, look! It is wanting to crawl.'

My god, there goes the stopper!
The cars in the Place de la Concorde——
Watch out!
A stampede, a stampede——

Horns twirling, and jungle gutterals.
An exploded bottle of stout,
Slack foam in the lap.
You stumble out,

Dwarf baby,
The knife in your back.
'I feel weak.'
The secret is out.

The Jailor

My night sweats grease his breakfast plate.
The same placard of blue fog is wheeled into position
With the same trees and headstones.
Is that all he can come up with,
The rattler of keys?

I have been drugged and raped.
Seven hours knocked out of my right mind
Into a black sack
Where I relax, foetus or cat,
Lever of his wet dreams.

Something is gone.
My sleeping capsule, my red and blue zeppelin
Drops me from a terrible altitude.
Carapace smashed,
I spread to the beaks of birds.

O little gimlets——
What holes this papery day is already full of!
He has been burning me with cigarettes,
Pretending I am a negress with pink paws.
I am myself. That is not enough.

The fever trickles and stiffens in my hair.
My ribs show. What have I eaten?
Lies and smiles.
Surely the sky is not that color,
Surely the grass should be rippling.

All day, gluing my church of burnt matchsticks,
I dream of someone else entirely.

And he, for this subversion
Hurts me, he
With his armory of fakery,

His high, cold masks of amnesia.
How did I get here?
Indeterminate criminal,
I die with variety——
Hung, starved, burned, hooked.

I imagine him
Impotent as distant thunder,
In whose shadow I have eaten my ghost ration.
I wish him dead or away.
That, it seems, is the impossibility.

That being free. What would the dark
Do without fevers to eat?
What would the light
Do without eyes to knife, what would he
Do, do, do without me.

Cut

for Susan O'Neill Roe

What a thrill——
My thumb instead of an onion.
The top quite gone
Except for a sort of a hinge

Of skin,
A flap like a hat,
Dead white.
Then that red plush.

Little pilgrim,
The Indian's axed your scalp.
Your turkey wattle
Carpet rolls

Straight from the heart.
I step on it,
Clutching my bottle
Of pink fizz.

A celebration, this is.
Out of a gap
A million soldiers run,
Redcoats, every one.

Whose side are they on?
O my
Homunculus, I am ill.
I have taken a pill to kill

The thin
Papery feeling.
Saboteur,
Kamikaze man——

The stain on your
Gauze Ku Klux Klan
Babushka
Darkens and tarnishes and when

The balled
Pulp of your heart
Confronts its small
Mill of silence

How you jump——
Trepanned veteran,
Dirty girl,
Thumb stump.

Elm

(for Ruth Fainlight)

I know the bottom, she says. I know it with my great tap root:
It is what you fear.
I do not fear it: I have been there.

Is it the sea you hear in me,
Its dissatisfactions?
Or the voice of nothing, that was your madness?

Love is a shadow.
How you lie and cry after it
Listen: these are its hooves: it has gone off, like a horse.

All night I shall gallop thus, impetuously,
Till your head is a stone, your pillow a little turf,
Echoing, echoing.

Or shall I bring you the sound of poisons?
This is rain now, this big hush.
And this is the fruit of it: tin-white, like arsenic.

I have suffered the atrocity of sunsets.
Scorched to the root
My red filaments burn and stand, a hand of wires.

Now I break up in pieces that fly about like clubs.
A wind of such violence
Will tolerate no bystanding: I must shriek.

The moon, also, is merciless: she would drag me
Cruelly, being barren.
Her radiance scathes me. Or perhaps I have caught her.

I let her go. I let her go
Diminished and flat, as after radical surgery.
How your bad dreams possess and endow me.

I am inhabited by a cry.
Nightly it flaps out
Looking, with its hooks, for something to love.

I am terrified by this dark thing
That sleeps in me;
All day I feel its soft, feathery turnings, its malignity.

Clouds pass and disperse.
Are those the faces of love, those pale irretrievables?
Is it for such I agitate my heart?

I am incapable of more knowledge.
What is this, this face
So murderous in its strangle of branches?——

Its snaky acids hiss.
It petrifies the will. These are the isolate, slow faults
That kill, that kill, that kill.

The Night Dances

A smile fell in the grass.
Irretrievable!

And how will your night dances
Lose themselves. In mathematics?

Such pure leaps and spirals——
Surely they travel

The world forever, I shall not entirely
Sit emptied of beauties, the gift

Of your small breath, the drenched grass
Smell of your sleeps, lilies, lilies.

Their flesh bears no relation.
Cold folds of ego, the calla,

And the tiger, embellishing itself——
Spots, and a spread of hot petals.

The comets
Have such a space to cross,

Such coldness, forgetfulness.
So your gestures flake off——

Warm and human, then their pink light
Bleeding and peeling

Through the black amnesias of heaven.
Why am I given

These lamps, these planets
Falling like blessings, like flakes

Six-sided, white
On my eyes, my lips, my hair

Touching and melting.
Nowhere.

The Detective

What was she doing when it blew in
Over the seven hills, the red furrow, the blue mountain?
Was she arranging cups? It is important.
Was she at the window, listening?
In that valley the train shrieks echo like souls on hooks.

That is the valley of death, though the cows thrive.
In her garden the lies were shaking out their moist silks
And the eyes of the killer moving sluglike and sidelong,
Unable to face the fingers, those egotists.
The fingers were tamping a woman into a wall,

A body into a pipe, and the smoke rising.
This is the smell of years burning, here in the kitchen,
These are the deceits, tacked up like family photographs,
And this is a man, look at his smile,
The death weapon? No-one is dead.

There is no body in the house at all.
There is the smell of polish, there are plush carpets.
There is the sunlight, playing its blades,
Bored hoodlum in a red room
Where the wireless talks to itself like an elderly relative.

Did it come like an arrow, did it come like a knife?
Which of the poisons is it?
Which of the nerve-curlers, the convulsors? Did it electrify?
This is a case without a body.
The body does not come into it at all.

It is a case of vaporization.
The mouth first, its absence reported

In the second year. It had been insatiable
And in punishment was hung out like brown fruit
To wrinkle and dry.

The breasts next.
These were harder, two white stones.
The milk came yellow, then blue and sweet as water.
There was no absence of lips, there were two children,
But their bones showed, and the moon smiled.

Then the dry wood, the gates,
The brown motherly furrows, the whole estate.
We walk on air, Watson.
There is only the moon, embalmed in phosphorus.
There is only a crow in a tree. Make notes.

Ariel

Stasis in darkness.
Then the substanceless blue
Pour of tor and distances.

God's lioness,
How one we grow,
Pivot of heels and knees!—The furrow

Splits and passes, sister to
The brown arc
Of the neck I cannot catch,

Nigger-eye
Berries cast dark
Hooks——

Black sweet blood mouthfuls,
Shadows.
Something else

Hauls me through air——
Thighs, hair;
Flakes from my heels.

White
Godiva, I unpeel——
Dead hands, dead stringencies.

And now I
Foam to wheat, a glitter of seas.
The child's cry

Melts in the wall.
And I
Am the arrow,

The dew that flies
Suicidal, at one with the drive
Into the red

Eye, the cauldron of morning.

Death & Co.

Two. Of course there are two.
It seems perfectly natural now——
The one who never looks up, whose eyes are lidded
And balled, like Blake's,
Who exhibits

The birthmarks that are his trademark——
The scald scar of water,
The nude
Verdigris of the condor.
I am red meat. His beak

Claps sidewise: I am not his yet.
He tells me how badly I photograph.
He tells me how sweet
The babies look in their hospital
Icebox, a simple

Frill at the neck,
Then the flutings of their Ionian
Death-gowns,
Then two little feet.
He does not smile or smoke.

The other does that,
His hair long and plausive.
Bastard
Masturbating a glitter,
He wants to be loved.

I do not stir.
The frost makes a flower,

The dew makes a star.
The dead bell,
The dead bell.

Somebody's done for.

Magi

The abstracts hover like dull angels:
Nothing so vulgar as a nose or an eye
Bossing the ethereal blanks of their face-ovals.

Their whiteness bears no relation to laundry,
Snow, chalk or suchlike. They're
The real thing, all right: the Good, the True——

Salutary and pure as boiled water,
Loveless as the multiplication table.
While the child smiles into thin air.

Six months in the world, and she is able
To rock on all fours like a padded hammock.
For her, the heavy notion of Evil

Attending her cot is less than a belly ache,
And Love the mother of milk, no theory.
They mistake their star, these papery godfolk.

They want the crib of some lamp-headed Plato.
Let them astound his heart with their merit.
What girl ever flourished in such company?

Lesbos

Viciousness in the kitchen!
The potatoes hiss.
It is all Hollywood, windowless,
The fluorescent light wincing on and off like a terrible migraine,
Coy paper strips for doors——
Stage curtains, a widow's frizz.
And I, love, am a pathological liar,
And my child—look at her, face down on the floor,
Little unstrung puppet, kicking to disappear——
Why she is a schizophrenic,
Her face red and white, a panic.
You have stuck her kittens outside your window
In a sort of cement well
Where they crap and puke and cry and she can't hear.
You say you can't stand her,
The bastard's a girl.
You who have blown your tubes like a bad radio
Clear of voices and history, the staticky
Noise of the new.
You say I should drown the kittens. Their smell!
You say I should drown my girl.
She'll cut her throat at ten if she's mad at two.
The baby smiles, fat snail,
From the polished lozenges of orange linoleum.
You could eat him. He's a boy.
You say your husband is just no good to you,
His Jew-mama guards his sweet sex like a pearl.
You have one baby, I have two.
I should sit on a rock off Cornwall and comb my hair.
I should wear tiger pants, I should have an affair.
We should meet in another life, we should meet in air,
Me and you.

Meanwhile there's a stink of fat and baby crap.
I'm doped and thick from my last sleeping pill.
The smog of cooking, the smog of hell
Floats our heads, two venomous opposites,
Our bones, our hair.
I call you Orphan, orphan. You are ill.
The sun gives you ulcers, the wind gives you t.b.
Once you were beautiful.
In New York, Hollywood, the men said: 'Through?
Gee baby, you are rare.'
You acted, acted, acted for the thrill.
The impotent husband slumps out for a coffee.
I try to keep him in,
An old pole for the lightning,
The acid baths, the skyfuls off of you.
He lumps it down the plastic cobbled hill,
Flogged trolley. The sparks are blue.
The blue sparks spill,
Splitting like quartz into a million bits.

O jewel. O valuable.
That night the moon
Dragged its blood bag, sick
Animal
Up over the harbor lights.
And then grew normal,
Hard and apart and white.
The scale-sheen on the sand scared me to death.
We kept picking up handfuls, loving it,
Working it like dough, a mulatto body,
The silk grits.
A dog picked up your doggy husband. They went on.

Now I am silent, hate
Up to my neck,

Thick, thick.
I do not speak.
I am packing the hard potatoes like good clothes,
I am packing the babies,
I am packing the sick cats.
O vase of acid,
It is love you are full of. You know who you hate.
He is hugging his ball and chain down by the gate
That opens to the sea
Where it drives in, white and black,
Then spews it back.
Every day you fill him with soul-stuff, like a pitcher.
You are so exhausted.
Your voice my ear-ring,
Flapping and sucking, blood-loving bat.
That is that. That is that.
You peer from the door,
Sad hag. 'Every woman's a whore.
I can't communicate.'

I see your cute décor
Close on you like the fist of a baby
Or an anemone, that sea
Sweetheart, that kleptomaniac.
I am still raw.
I say I may be back.
You know what lies are for.

Even in your Zen heaven we shan't meet.

The Other

You come in late, wiping your lips.
What did I leave untouched on the doorstep——

White Nike,
Streaming between my walls?

Smilingly, blue lightning
Assumes, like a meathook, the burden of his parts.

The police love you, you confess everything.
Bright hair, shoe-black, old plastic,

Is my life so intriguing?
Is it for this you widen your eye-rings?

Is it for this the air motes depart?
They are not air motes, they are corpuscles.

Open your handbag. What is that bad smell?
It is your knitting, busily

Hooking itself to itself,
It is your sticky candies.

I have your head on my wall.
Navel cords, blue-red and lucent,

Shriek from my belly like arrows, and these I ride.
O moon-glow, o sick one,

The stolen horses, the fornications
Circle a womb of marble.

Where are you going
That you suck breath like mileage?

Sulfurous adulteries grieve in a dream.
Cold glass, how you insert yourself

Between myself and myself.
I scratch like a cat.

The blood that runs is dark fruit——
An effect, a cosmetic.

You smile.
No, it is not fatal.

Stopped Dead

A squeal of brakes.
Or is it a birth cry?
And here we are, hung out over the dead drop
Uncle, pants factory Fatso, millionaire.
And you out cold beside me in your chair.

The wheels, two rubber grubs, bite their sweet tails.
Is that Spain down there?
Red and yellow, two passionate hot metals
Writhing and sighing, what sort of a scenery is it?
It isn't England, it isn't France, it isn't Ireland.

It's violent. We're here on a visit,
With a goddam baby screaming off somewhere.
There's always a bloody baby in the air.
I'd call it a sunset, but
Whoever heard a sunset yowl like that?

You are sunk in your seven chins, still as a ham.
Who do you think I am,
Uncle, uncle?
Sad Hamlet, with a knife?
Where do you stash your life?

Is it a penny, a pearl——
Your soul, your soul?
I'll carry it off like a rich pretty girl,
Simply open the door and step out of the car
And live in Gibraltar on air, on air.

Poppies in October

for Helder and Suzette Macedo

Even the sun-clouds this morning cannot manage such skirts.
Nor the woman in the ambulance
Whose red heart blooms through her coat so astoundingly——

A gift, a love gift
Utterly unasked for
By a sky

Palely and flamily
Igniting its carbon monoxides, by eyes
Dulled to a halt under bowlers.

O my God, what am I
That these late mouths should cry open
In a forest of frost, in a dawn of cornflowers!

The Courage of Shutting-Up

The courage of the shut mouth, in spite of artillery!
The line pink and quiet, a worm, basking.
There are black discs behind it, the discs of outrage,
And the outrage of a sky, the lined brain of it.
The discs revolve, they ask to be heard,

Loaded, as they are, with accounts of bastardies.
Bastardies, usages, desertions and doubleness,
The needle journeying in its groove,
Silver beast between two dark canyons,
A great surgeon, now a tattooist,

Tattooing over and over the same blue grievances,
The snakes, the babies, the tits
On mermaids and two-legged dreamgirls.
The surgeon is quiet, he does not speak.
He has seen too much death, his hands are full of it.

So the discs of the brain revolve, like the muzzles of cannon.
Then there is that antique billhook, the tongue,
Indefatigable, purple. Must it be cut out?
It has nine tails, it is dangerous.
And the noise it flays from the air, once it gets going.

No, the tongue, too, has been put by
Hung up in the library with the engravings of Rangoon
And the fox heads, the otter heads, the heads of dead rabbits.
It is a marvellous object——
The things it has pierced in its time!

But how about the eyes, the eyes, the eyes?
Mirrors can kill and talk, they are terrible rooms

In which a torture goes on one can only watch.
The face that lived in this mirror is the face of a dead man.
Do not worry about the eyes——

They may be white and shy, they are no stool pigeons,
Their death rays folded like flags
Of a country no longer heard of,
An obstinate independency
Insolvent among the mountains.

Nick and the Candlestick

I am a miner. The light burns blue.
Waxy stalacmites
Drip and thicken, tears

The earthen womb
Exudes from its dead boredom.
Black bat airs

Wrap me, raggy shawls,
Cold homicides.
They weld to me like plums.

Old cave of calcium
Icicles, old echoer.
Even the newts are white,

Those holy Joes.
And the fish, the fish——
Christ! they are panes of ice,

A vice of knives,
A piranha
Religion, drinking

Its first communion out of my live toes.
The candle
Gulps and recovers its small altitude,

Its yellows hearten.
O love, how did you get here?
O embryo

Remembering, even in sleep,
Your crossed position.
The blood blooms clean

In you, ruby.
The pain
You wake to is not yours.

Love, love,
I have hung our cave with roses,
With soft rugs——

The last of Victoriana.
Let the stars
Plummet to their dark address,

Let the mercuric
Atoms that cripple drip
Into the terrible well,

You are the one
Solid the spaces lean on, envious.
You are the baby in the barn.

Berck-Plage

(1)

This is the sea, then, this great abeyance.
How the sun's poultice draws on my inflammation!

Electrifyingly-colored sherbets, scooped from the freeze
By pale girls, travel the air in scorched hands.

Why is it so quiet, what are they hiding?
I have two legs, and I move smilingly.

A sandy damper kills the vibrations;
It stretches for miles, the shrunk voices

Waving and crutchless, half their old size.
The lines of the eye, scalded by these bald surfaces,

Boomerang like anchored elastics, hurting the owner.
Is it any wonder he puts on dark glasses?

Is it any wonder he affects a black cassock?
Here he comes now, among the mackerel gatherers

Who wall up their backs against him.
They are handling the black and green lozenges like the parts
of a body.

The sea, that crystallized these,
Creeps away, many-snaked, with a long hiss of distress.

This black boot has no mercy for anybody.
Why should it, it is the hearse of a dead foot,

The high, dead, toeless foot of this priest
Who plumbs the well of his book,

The bent print bulging before him like scenery.
Obscene bikinis hide in the dunes,

Breasts and hips a confectioner's sugar
Of little crystals, titillating the light,

While a green pool opens its eye,
Sick with what it has swallowed——

Limbs, images, shrieks. Behind the concrete bunkers
Two lovers unstick themselves.

O white sea-crockery,
What cupped sighs, what salt in the throat!

And the onlooker, trembling,
Drawn like a long material

Through a still virulence,
And a weed, hairy as privates.

(3)

On the balconies of the hotel, things are glittering.
Things, things——

Tubular steel wheelchairs, aluminum crutches.
Such salt-sweetness. Why should I walk

Beyond the breakwater, spotty with barnacles?
I am not a nurse, white and attendant,

I am not a smile.
These children are after something, with hooks and cries,

And my heart too small to bandage their terrible faults.
This is the side of a man: his red ribs,

The nerves bursting like trees, and this is the surgeon:
One mirrory eye——

A facet of knowledge.
On a striped mattress in one room

An old man is vanishing.
There is no help in his weeping wife.

Where are the eye-stones, yellow and valuable,
And the tongue, sapphire of ash.

(4)

A wedding-cake face in a paper frill.
How superior he is now.

It is like possessing a saint.
The nurses in their wing-caps are no longer so beautiful;

They are browning, like touched gardenias.
The bed is rolled from the wall.

This is what it is to be complete. It is horrible.
Is he wearing pajamas or an evening suit

Under the glued sheet from which his powdery beak
Rises so whitely, unbuffeted?

They propped his jaw with a book until it stiffened
And folded his hands, that were shaking: goodbye, goodbye.

Now the washed sheets fly in the sun,
The pillow cases are sweetening.

It is a blessing, it is a blessing:
The long coffin of soap-colored oak,

The curious bearers and the raw date
Engraving itself in silver with marvelous calm.

(5)

The grey sky lowers, the hills like a green sea
Run fold upon fold far off, concealing their hollows,

The hollows in which rock the thoughts of the wife——
Blunt, practical boats

Full of dresses and hats and china and married daughters.
In the parlor of the stone house

One curtain is flickering from the open window,
Flickering and pouring, a pitiful candle.

This is the tongue of the dead man: remember, remember.
How far he is now, his actions

Around him like livingroom furniture, like a décor.
As the pallors gather——

The pallors of hands and neighborly faces,
The elate pallors of flying iris.

They are flying off into nothing: remember us.
The empty benches of memory look over stones,

Marble façades with blue veins, and jelly-glassfuls of daffodils.
It is so beautiful up here: it is a stopping place.

(6)

The unnatural fatness of these lime leaves!——
Pollarded green balls, the trees march to church.

The voice of the priest, in thin air,
Meets the corpse at the gate,

Addressing it, while the hills roll the notes of the dead bell;
A glitter of wheat and crude earth.

What is the name of that color?——
Old blood of caked walls the sun heals,

Old blood of limb stumps, burnt hearts.
The widow with her black pocketbook and three daughters,

Necessary among the flowers,
Enfolds her face like fine linen,

Not to be spread again.
While a sky, wormy with put-by smiles,

Passes cloud after cloud.
And the bride flowers expend a freshness,

And the soul is a bride
In a still place, and the groom is red and forgetful, he is featureless.

(7)

Behind the glass of this car
The world purrs, shut-off and gentle.

And I am dark-suited and still, a member of the party,
Gliding up in low gear behind the cart.

And the priest is a vessel,
A tarred fabric, sorry and dull,

Following the coffin on its flowery cart like a beautiful woman,
A crest of breasts, eyelids and lips

Storming the hilltop.
Then, from the barred yard, the children

Smell the melt of shoe-blacking,
Their faces turning, wordless and slow,

Their eyes opening
On a wonderful thing——

Six round black hats in the grass and a lozenge of wood,
And a naked mouth, red and awkward.

For a minute the sky pours into the hole like plasma.
There is no hope, it is given up.

Gulliver

Over your body the clouds go
High, high and icily
And a little flat, as if they

Floated on a glass that was invisible.
Unlike swans,
Having no reflections;

Unlike you,
With no strings attached.
All cool, all blue. Unlike you——

You, there on your back,
Eyes to the sky.
The spider-men have caught you,

Winding and twining their petty fetters,
Their bribes——
So many silks.

How they hate you.
They converse in the valley of your fingers, they are inchworms.
They would have you sleep in their cabinets,

This toe and that toe, a relic.
Step off!
Step off seven leagues, like those distances

That revolve in Crivelli, untouchable.
Let this eye be an eagle,
The shadow of his lip, an abyss.

Getting There

How far is it?
How far is it now?
The gigantic gorilla interior
Of the wheels move, they appal me——
The terrible brains
Of Krupp, black muzzles
Revolving, the sound
Punching out Absence! like cannon.
It is Russia I have to get across, it is some war or other.
I am dragging my body
Quietly through the straw of the boxcars.
Now is the time for bribery.
What do wheels eat, these wheels
Fixed to their arcs like gods,
The silver leash of the will——
Inexorable. And their pride!
All the gods know is destinations.
I am a letter in this slot——
I fly to a name, two eyes.
Will there be fire, will there be bread?
Here there is such mud.
It is a trainstop, the nurses
Undergoing the faucet water, its veils, veils in a nunnery,
Touching their wounded,
The men the blood still pumps forward,
Legs, arms piled outside
The tent of unending cries——
A hospital of dolls.
And the men, what is left of the men
Pumped ahead by these pistons, this blood
Into the next mile,

The next hour——
Dynasty of broken arrows!

How far is it?
There is mud on my feet,
Thick, red and slipping. It is Adam's side,
This earth I rise from, and I in agony.
I cannot undo myself, and the train is steaming.
Steaming and breathing, its teeth
Ready to roll, like a devil's.
There is a minute at the end of it
A minute, a dewdrop.
How far is it?
It is so small
The place I am getting to, why are there these obstacles——
The body of this woman,
Charred skirts and deathmask
Mourned by religious figures, by garlanded children.
And now detonations——
Thunder and guns.
The fire's between us.
Is there no still place
Turning and turning in the middle air,
Untouched and untouchable.
The train is dragging itself, it is screaming——
An animal
Insane for the destination,
The bloodspot,
The face at the end of the flare.
I shall bury the wounded like pupas,
I shall count and bury the dead.
Let their souls writhe in a dew,
Incense in my track.
The carriages rock, they are cradles.

And I, stepping from this skin
Of old bandages, boredoms, old faces

Step to you from the black car of Lethe,
Pure as a baby.

Medusa

Off that landspit of stony mouth-plugs,
Eyes rolled by white sticks,
Ears cupping the sea's incoherences,
You house your unnerving head—God-ball,
Lens of mercies,

Your stooges
Plying their wild cells in my keel's shadow,
Pushing by like hearts,
Red stigmata at the very center,
Riding the rip tide to the nearest point of departure,

Dragging their Jesus hair.
Did I escape, I wonder?
My mind winds to you,
Old barnacled umbilicus, Atlantic cable,
Keeping itself, it seems, in a state of miraculous repair.

In any case, you are always there,
Tremulous breath at the end of my line,
Curve of water upleaping
To my water rod, dazzling and grateful,
Touching and sucking.

I didn't call you.
I didn't call you at all.
Nevertheless, nevertheless
You steamed to me over the sea,
Fat and red, a placenta

Paralyzing the kicking lovers.
Cobra light

Squeezing the breath from the blood bells
Of the fuchsia. I could draw no breath,
Dead and moneyless,

Overexposed, like an X ray.
Who do you think you are?
A Communion wafer? Blubbery Mary?
I shall take no bite of your body,
Bottle in which I live,

Ghastly Vatican.
I am sick to death of hot salt.
Green as eunuchs, your wishes
Hiss at my sins.
Off, off, eely tentacle!

There is nothing between us.

Purdah

Jade——
Stone of the side,
The agonized

Side of green Adam, I
Smile, cross-legged,
Enigmatical,

Shifting my clarities.
So valuable.
How the sun polishes this shoulder!

And should
The moon, my
Indefatigable cousin

Rise, with her cancerous pallors,
Dragging trees——
Little bushy polyps,

Little nets,
My visibilities hide.
I gleam like a mirror.

At this facet the bridegroom arrives,
Lord of the mirrors.
It is himself he guides

In among these silk
Screens, these rustling appurtenances.
I breathe, and the mouth

Veil stirs its curtain.
My eye
Veil is

A concatenation of rainbows.
I am his.
Even in his

Absence, I
Revolve in my
Sheath of impossibles,

Priceless and quiet
Among these parakeets, macaws.
O chatterers

Attendants of the eyelash!
I shall unloose
One feather, like the peacock.

Attendants of the lip!
I shall unloose
One note

Shattering
The chandelier
Of air that all day plies

Its crystals,
A million ignorants.
Attendants!

Attendants!
And at his next step
I shall unloose

I shall unloose——
From the small jeweled
Doll he guards like a heart——

The lioness,
The shriek in the bath,
The cloak of holes.

The Moon and the Yew Tree

This is the light of the mind, cold and planetary.
The trees of the mind are black. The light is blue.
The grasses unload their griefs on my feet as if I were God,
Prickling my ankles and murmuring of their humility.
Fumey, spiritous mists inhabit this place
Separated from my house by a row of headstones.
I simply cannot see where there is to get to.

The moon is no door. It is a face in its own right,
White as a knuckle and terribly upset.
It drags the sea after it like a dark crime; it is quiet
With the O-gape of complete despair. I live here.
Twice on Sunday, the bells startle the sky——
Eight great tongues affirming the Resurrection.
At the end, they soberly bong out their names.

The yew tree points up. It has a Gothic shape.
The eyes lift after it and find the moon.
The moon is my mother. She is not sweet like Mary.
Her blue garments unloose small bats and owls.
How I would like to believe in tenderness——
The face of the effigy, gentled by candles,
Bending, on me in particular, its mild eyes.

I have fallen a long way. Clouds are flowering
Blue and mystical over the face of the stars.
Inside the church, the saints will be all blue,
Floating on their delicate feet over the cold pews,
Their hands and faces stiff with holiness.
The moon sees nothing of this. She is bald and wild.
And the message of the yew tree is blackness—blackness and silence.

A Birthday Present

What is this, behind this veil, is it ugly, is it beautiful?
It is shimmering, has it breasts, has it edges?

I am sure it is unique, I am sure it is just what I want.
When I am quiet at my cooking I feel it looking, I feel it thinking

'Is this the one I am to appear for,
Is this the elect one, the one with black eye-pits and a scar?

Measuring the flour, cutting off the surplus,
Adhering to rules, to rules, to rules.

Is this the one for the annunciation?
My god, what a laugh!'

But it shimmers, it does not stop, and I think it wants me.
I would not mind if it was bones, or a pearl button.

I do not want much of a present, anyway, this year.
After all, I am alive only by accident.

I would have killed myself gladly that time any possible way.
Now there are these veils, shimmering like curtains,

The diaphanous satins of a January window
White as babies' bedding and glittering with dead breath. O ivory!

It must be a tusk there, a ghost-column.
Can you not see I do not mind what it is.

Can you not give it to me?
Do not be ashamed—I do not mind if it is small.

Do not be mean, I am ready for enormity.
Let us sit down to it, one on either side, admiring the gleam,

The glaze, the mirrory variety of it.
Let us eat our last supper at it, like a hospital plate.

I know why you will not give it to me,
You are terrified

The world will go up in a shriek, and your head with it,
Bossed, brazen, an antique shield,

A marvel to your great-grandchildren.
Do not be afraid, it is not so.

I will only take it and go aside quietly.
You will not even hear me opening it, no paper crackle,

No falling ribbons, no scream at the end.
I do not think you credit me with this discretion.

If you only knew how the veils were killing my days.
To you they are only transparencies, clear air.

But my god, the clouds are like cotton——
Armies of them. They are carbon monoxide.

Sweetly, sweetly I breathe in,
Filling my veins with invisibles, with the million

Probable motes that tick the years off my life.
You are silver-suited for the occasion. O adding machine——

Is it impossible for you to let something go and have it go whole?
Must you stamp each piece in purple,

Must you kill what you can?
There is this one thing I want today, and only you can give it to me.

It stands at my window, big as the sky.
It breathes from my sheets, the cold, dead center

Where spilt lives congeal and stiffen to history.
Let it not come by the mail, finger by finger.

Let it not come by word of mouth, I should be sixty
By the time the whole of it was delivered, and too numb to use it.

Only let down the veil, the veil, the veil.
If it were death

I would admire the deep gravity of it, its timeless eyes.
I would know you were serious.

There would be a nobility then, there would be a birthday.
And the knife not carve, but enter

Pure and clean as the cry of a baby,
And the universe slide from my side.

Letter in November

Love, the world
Suddenly turns, turns color. The streetlight
Splits through the rat's-tail
Pods of the laburnum at nine in the morning.
It is the Arctic,

This little black
Circle, with its tawn silk grasses—babies' hair.
There is a green in the air,
Soft, delectable.
It cushions me lovingly.

I am flushed and warm.
I think I may be enormous,
I am so stupidly happy,
My Wellingtons
Squelching and squelching through the beautiful red.

This is my property.
Two times a day
I pace it, sniffing
The barbarous holly with its viridian
Scallops, pure iron,

And the wall of old corpses.
I love them.
I love them like history.
The apples are golden,
Imagine it——

My seventy trees
Holding their gold-ruddy balls

In a thick grey death-soup,
Their million
Gold leaves metal and breathless.

O love, O celibate.
Nobody but me
Walks the waist-high wet.
The irreplaceable
Golds bleed and deepen, the mouths of Thermopylae.

Amnesiac

No use, no use, now, begging Recognize.
There is nothing to do with such a beautiful blank but smooth it.
Name, house, car keys,

The little toy wife
Erased, sigh, sigh.
Four babies and a cocker.

Nurses the size of worms and a minute doctor
Tuck him in.
Old happenings

Peel from his skin.
Down the drain with all of it!
Hugging his pillow

Like the red-headed sister he never dared to touch,
He dreams of a new one——
Barren, the lot are barren.

And of another color.
How they'll travel, travel, travel, scenery
Sparking off their brother-sister rears,

A comet tail.
And money the sperm fluid of it all.
One nurse brings in

A green drink, one a blue.
They rise on either side of him like stars.
The two drinks flame and foam.

O sister, mother, wife,
Sweet Lethe is my life.
I am never, never, never coming home!

The Rival

If the moon smiled, she would resemble you.
You leave the same impression
Of something beautiful, but annihilating.
Both of you are great light borrowers.
Her O-mouth grieves at the world; yours is unaffected,

And your first gift is making stone out of everything.
I wake to a mausoleum; you are here,
Ticking your fingers on the marble table, looking for cigarettes,
Spiteful as a woman, but not so nervous,
And dying to say something unanswerable.

The moon, too, abases her subjects,
But in the daytime she is ridiculous.
Your dissatisfactions, on the other hand,
Arrive through the mailslot with loving regularity,
White and blank, expansive as carbon monoxide.

No day is safe from news of you,
Walking about in Africa maybe, but thinking of me.

Daddy

You do not do, you do not do
Any more, black shoe
In which I have lived like a foot
For thirty years, poor and white,
Barely daring to breathe or Achoo.

Daddy, I have had to kill you.
You died before I had time——
Marble-heavy, a bag full of God,
Ghastly statue with one grey toe
Big as a Frisco seal

And a head in the freakish Atlantic
Where it pours bean green over blue
In the waters off beautiful Nauset.
I used to pray to recover you.
Ach, du.

In the German tongue, in the Polish town
Scraped flat by the roller
Of wars, wars, wars.
But the name of the town is common.
My Polack friend

Says there are a dozen or two.
So I never could tell where you
Put your foot, your root,
I never could talk to you.
The tongue stuck in my jaw.

It stuck in a barb wire snare.
Ich, ich, ich, ich.

I could hardly speak.
I thought every German was you.
And the language obscene

An engine, an engine
Chuffing me off like a Jew.
A Jew to Dachau, Auschwitz, Belsen.
I began to talk like a Jew.
I think I may well be a Jew.

The snows of the Tyrol, the clear beer of Vienna
Are not very pure or true.
With my gypsy ancestress and my weird luck
And my Taroc pack and my Taroc pack
I may be a bit of a Jew.

I have always been scared of *you,*
With your Luftwaffe, your gobbledygoo.
And your neat moustache
And your Aryan eye, bright blue.
Panzer-man, panzer-man, o You——

Not God but a swastika
So black no sky could squeak through.
Every woman adores a Fascist,
The boot in the face, the brute
Brute heart of a brute like you.

You stand at the blackboard, daddy,
In the picture I have of you,
A cleft in your chin instead of your foot
But no less a devil for that, no not
Any less the black man who

Bit my pretty red heart in two.
I was ten when they buried you.
At twenty I tried to die
And get back, back, back to you.
I thought even the bones would do

But they pulled me out of the sack,
And they stuck me together with glue.
And then I knew what to do.
I made a model of you,
A man in black with a Meinkampf look

And a love of the rack and the screw.
And I said I do, I do.
So daddy, I'm finally through.
The black telephone's off at the root,
The voices just can't worm through.

If I've killed one man, I've killed two——
The vampire who said he was you
And drank my blood for a year,
Seven years, if you want to know.
Daddy, you can lie back now.

There's a stake in your fat black heart
And the villagers never liked you.
They are dancing and stamping on you.
They always *knew* it was you.
Daddy, daddy, you bastard, I'm through.

You're

Clownlike, happiest on your hands,
Feet to the stars, and moon-skulled,
Gilled like a fish. A common-sense
Thumbs-down on the dodo's mode.
Wrapped up in yourself like a spool,
Trawling your dark as owls do.
Mute as a turnip from the Fourth
Of July to All Fools' Day,
O high-riser, my little loaf.

Vague as fog and looked for like mail.
Farther off than Australia.
Bent-backed Atlas, our traveled prawn.
Snug as a bud and at home
Like a sprat in a pickle jug.
A creel of eels, all ripples.
Jumpy as a Mexican bean.
Right, like a well-done sum.
A clean slate, with your own face on.

Fever 103°

Pure? What does it mean?
The tongues of hell
Are dull, dull as the triple

Tongues of dull, fat Cerberus
Who wheezes at the gate. Incapable
Of licking clean

The aguey tendon, the sin, the sin.
The tinder cries.
The indelible smell

Of a snuffed candle!
Love, love, the low smokes roll
From me like Isadora's scarves, I'm in a fright

One scarf will catch and anchor in the wheel.
Such yellow sullen smokes
Make their own element. They will not rise,

But trundle round the globe
Choking the aged and the meek,
The weak

Hothouse baby in its crib,
The ghastly orchid
Hanging its hanging garden in the air,

Devilish leopard!
Radiation turned it white
And killed it in an hour.

Greasing the bodies of adulterers
Like Hiroshima ash and eating in.
The sin. The sin.

Darling, all night
I have been flickering, off, on, off, on.
The sheets grow heavy as a lecher's kiss.

Three days. Three nights.
Lemon water, chicken
Water, water make me retch.

I am too pure for you or anyone.
Your body
Hurts me as the world hurts God. I am a lantern——

My head a moon
Of Japanese paper, my gold beaten skin
Infinitely delicate and infinitely expensive.

Does not my heat astound you. And my light.
All by myself I am a huge camellia
Glowing and coming and going, flush on flush.

I think I am going up,
I think I may rise——
The beads of hot metal fly, and I, love, I

Am a pure acetylene
Virgin
Attended by roses,

By kisses, by cherubim,
By whatever these pink things mean.
Not you, nor him

Nor him, nor him
(My selves dissolving, old whore petticoats)——
To Paradise.

The Bee Meeting

Who are these people at the bridge to meet me? They are the villagers——
The rector, the midwife, the sexton, the agent for bees.
In my sleeveless summery dress I have no protection,
And they are all gloved and covered, why did nobody tell me?
They are smiling and taking out veils tacked to ancient hats.

I am nude as a chicken neck, does nobody love me?
Yes, here is the secretary of bees with her white shop smock,
Buttoning the cuffs at my wrists and the slit from my neck to my knees.
Now I am milkweed silk, the bees will not notice.
They will not smell my fear, my fear, my fear.

Which is the rector now, is it that man in black?
Which is the midwife, is that her blue coat?
Everybody is nodding a square black head, they are knights in visors,
Breastplates of cheesecloth knotted under the armpits.
Their smiles and their voices are changing. I am led through a beanfield,

Strips of tinfoil winking like people,
Feather dusters fanning their hands in a sea of bean flowers,
Creamy bean flowers with black eyes and leaves like bored hearts.
Is it blood clots the tendrils are dragging up that string?
No, no, it is scarlet flowers that will one day be edible.

Now they are giving me a fashionable white straw Italian hat
And a black veil that molds to my face, they are making me one of them.
They are leading me to the shorn grove, the circle of hives.
Is it the hawthorn that smells so sick?
The barren body of hawthorn, etherizing its children.

Is it some operation that is taking place?
It is the surgeon my neighbors are waiting for,

This apparition in a green helmet,
Shining gloves and white suit.
Is it the butcher, the grocer, the postman, someone I know?

I cannot run, I am rooted, and the gorse hurts me
With its yellow purses, its spiky armory.
I could not run without having to run forever.
The white hive is snug as a virgin,
Sealing off her brood cells, her honey, and quietly humming.

Smoke rolls and scarves in the grove.
The mind of the hive thinks this is the end of everything.
Here they come, the outriders, on their hysterical elastics.
If I stand very still, they will think I am cow parsley,
A gullible head untouched by their animosity,

Not even nodding, a personage in a hedgerow.
The villagers open the chambers, they are hunting the queen.
Is she hiding, is she eating honey? She is very clever.
She is old, old, old, she must live another year, and she knows it.
While in their fingerjoint cells the new virgins

Dream of a duel they will win inevitably,
A curtain of wax dividing them from the bride flight,
The upflight of the murderess into a heaven that loves her.
The villagers are moving the virgins, there will be no killing.
The old queen does not show herself, is she so ungrateful?

I am exhausted, I am exhausted——
Pillar of white in a blackout of knives.
I am the magician's girl who does not flinch.
The villagers are untying their disguises, they are shaking hands.
Whose is that long white box in the grove, what have they accomplished,
        why am I cold.

The Arrival of the Bee Box

I ordered this, this clean wood box
Square as a chair and almost too heavy to lift.
I would say it was the coffin of a midget
Or a square baby
Were there not such a din in it.

The box is locked, it is dangerous.
I have to live with it overnight
And I can't keep away from it.
There are no windows, so I can't see what is in there.
There is only a little grid, no exit.

I put my eye to the grid.
It is dark, dark,
With the swarmy feeling of African hands
Minute and shrunk for export,
Black on black, angrily clambering.

How can I let them out?
It is the noise that appals me most of all,
The unintelligible syllables.
It is like a Roman mob,
Small, taken one by one, but my god, together!

I lay my ear to furious Latin.
I am not a Caesar.
I have simply ordered a box of maniacs.
They can be sent back.
They can die, I need feed them nothing, I am the owner.

I wonder how hungry they are.
I wonder if they would forget me

If I just undid the locks and stood back and turned into a tree.
There is the laburnum, its blond colonnades,
And the petticoats of the cherry.

They might ignore me immediately
In my moon suit and funeral veil.
I am no source of honey
So why should they turn on me?
Tomorrow I will be sweet God, I will set them free.

The box is only temporary.

Stings

Bare-handed, I hand the combs.
The man in white smiles, bare-handed,
Our cheesecloth gauntlets neat and sweet,
The throats of our wrists brave lilies.
He and I

Have a thousand clean cells between us,
Eight combs of yellow cups,
And the hive itself a teacup,
White with pink flowers on it.
With excessive love I enameled it

Thinking 'Sweetness, sweetness.'
Brood cells grey as the fossils of shells
Terrify me, they seem so old.
What am I buying, wormy mahogany?
Is there any queen at all in it?

If there is, she is old,
Her wings torn shawls, her long body
Rubbed of its plush——
Poor and bare and unqueenly and even shameful.
I stand in a column

Of winged, unmiraculous women,
Honey-drudgers.
I am no drudge
Though for years I have eaten dust
And dried plates with my dense hair.

And seen my strangeness evaporate,
Blue dew from dangerous skin.
Will they hate me,
These women who only scurry,
Whose news is the open cherry, the open clover?

It is almost over.
I am in control.
Here is my honey-machine,
It will work without thinking,
Opening, in spring, like an industrious virgin

To scour the creaming crests
As the moon, for its ivory powders, scours the sea.
A third person is watching.
He has nothing to do with the bee-seller or with me.
Now he is gone

In eight great bounds, a great scapegoat.
Here is his slipper, here is another,
And here the square of white linen
He wore instead of a hat.
He was sweet,

The sweat of his efforts a rain
Tugging the world to fruit.
The bees found him out,
Molding onto his lips like lies,
Complicating his features.

They thought death was worth it, but I
Have a self to recover, a queen.
Is she dead, is she sleeping?
Where has she been,
With her lion-red body, her wings of glass?

Now she is flying
More terrible than she ever was, red
Scar in the sky, red comet
Over the engine that killed her—
The mausoleum, the wax house.

Wintering

This is the easy time, there is nothing doing.
I have whirled the midwife's extractor,
I have my honey,
Six jars of it,
Six cat's eyes in the wine cellar,

Wintering in a dark without window
At the heart of the house
Next to the last tenant's rancid jam
And the bottles of empty glitters——
Sir So-and-so's gin.

This is the room I have never been in.
This is the room I could never breathe in.
The black bunched in there like a bat,
No light
But the torch and its faint

Chinese yellow on appalling objects——
Black asininity. Decay.
Possession.
It is they who own me.
Neither cruel nor indifferent,

Only ignorant.
This is the time of hanging on for the bees——the bees
So slow I hardly know them,
Filing like soldiers
To the syrup tin

To make up for the honey I've taken.
Tate and Lyle keeps them going,

The refined snow.
It is Tate and Lyle they live on, instead of flowers.
They take it. The cold sets in.

Now they ball in a mass,
Black
Mind against all that white.
The smile of the snow is white.
It spreads itself out, a mile-long body of Meissen,

Into which, on warm days,
They can only carry their dead.
The bees are all women,
Maids and the long royal lady.
They have got rid of the men,

The blunt, clumsy stumblers, the boors.
Winter is for women——
The woman, still at her knitting,
At the cradle of Spanish walnut,
Her body a bulb in the cold and too dumb to think.

Will the hive survive, will the gladiolas
Succeed in banking their fires
To enter another year?
What will they taste of, the Christmas roses?
The bees are flying. They taste the spring.

II

Facsimile of the manuscript
for *Ariel and other poems*

ARIEL

and other poems

by

Sylvia Plath

DADDY

and other poems

by

Sylvia Plath

DADDY

and other poems

by

Sylvia Plath

for

Frieda and Nicholas

MORNING SONG
THE COURIERS   •
THE RABBIT CATCHER
THALIDOMIDE
THE APPLICANT
BARREN WOMAN
LADY LAZARUS
TULIPS
A SECRET
THE JAILOR
— CUT
ELM
THE NIGHT DANCES
THE DETECTIVE
ARIEL
MAGI ← DEATH & CO.
LESBOS
— THE OTHER
STOPPED DEAD
POPPIES IN OCTOBER
THE COURAGE OF ~~QUIETNESS~~ Shutting-Up
NICK AND THE CANDLESTICK
BERCK-PLAGE
GULLIVER
GETTING THERE
MEDUSA
PURDAH
THE MOON AND THE YEW TREE
A BIRTHDAY PRESENT
LETTER IN NOVEMBER
AMNESIAC
THE RIVAL
DADDY
YOU'RE
FEVER 103°
THE BEE MEETING
THE ARRIVAL OF THE BEE BOX
STINGS
(THE SWARM)
WINTERING

MORNING SONG: Obs:Partisan Rev:BBC:Hutchinson Anth:

THE COURIERS: London Mag

THE RABBIT CATCHER:Obs:BBC:

THALIDOMIDE:

THE APPLICANT: London Mag:

BARREN WOMAN: London Mag:

LADY LAZARUS:

TULIPS: New Yorker: Mermaid Festival 1961: PEN 1963

A SECRET:

THE JAILOR:

CUT: London Mag

ELM: New Yorker:

THE NIGHT DANCES:

THE DETECTIVE:

ARIEL: Observer:
         DEATH & CO.:

MAGI: New Statesman:

LESBOS:

THE OTHER:

STOPPED DEAD: London Mag:

POPPIES IN OCTOBER: Observer:

THE COURAGE OF QUIETNESS:

NICK AND THE CANDLESTICK:

BERCK-PLAGE :BBC: London Mag

GULLIVER:

GETTING THERE:

MEDUSA:

PURDAH : Poetry

THE MOON AND THE YEW TREE :New Yorker:BBC:PEN 1963:

A BIRTHDAY PRESENT:

LETTER IN NOVEMBER : London mag

AMNESIAC : New Yorker

THE RIVAL :Obs:

DADDY:

YOU'RE : Harper's:London Mag:BBC:

FEVER 103° : Poetry

THE BEE MEETING : London Mag

THE ARRIVAL OF THE BEE BOX: Atlantic Monthly

STINGS : London Mag

(THE SWARM)

WINTERING: Atlantic Monthly

Morning Song

Love set you going like a fat gold watch.
The midwife slapped your footsoles, and your bald cry
Took its place among the elements.

Our voices echo, magnifying your arrival. New statue
In a drafty museum, your nakedness
Shadows our safety. We stand round blankly as walls.

I'm no more your mother
Than the cloud that distils a mirror to reflect its own slow
Effacement at the wind's hand.

All night your moth-breath
Flickers among the flat pink roses. I wake to listen:
A far sea moves in my ear.

One cry, and I stumble from bed, cow-heavy and floral
In my Victorian nightgown.
Your mouth opens clean as a cat's. The window square

Whitens and swallows its dull stars. And now you try
Your handful of notes;
The clear vowels rise like balloons.

The Couriers

The word of a snail on the plate of a leaf?
It is not mine. Do not accept it.

Acetic acid in a sealed tin?
Do not accept it. It is not genuine.

A ring of gold with the sun in it?
Lies. Lies and a grief.

Frost on a leaf, the immaculate
Cauldron, talking and crackling

All to itself on the top of each
Of nine black Alps,

A disturbance in mirrors,
The sea shattering its grey one---

Love, love, my season.

The Rabbit Catcher

It was a place of force---
The wind gagging my mouth with my own blown hair,
Tearing off my voice, and the sea
Blinding me with its lights, the lives of the dead
Unreeling in it, spreading like oil.

I tasted the malignity of the gorse,
Its black spikes,
The extreme unction of its yellow candle-flowers.
They had an efficiency, a great beauty,
And were extravagant, like torture.

There was only one place to get to.
Simmering, perfumed,
The paths narrowed into the hollow.
And the snares almost effaced themselves---
Zeroes, shutting on nothing,

Set close, like birth pangs.
The absence of shrieks
Made a hole in the hot day, a vacancy.
The glassy light was a clear wall,
The thickets quiet.

I felt a still busyness, an intent.
I felt hands round a tea mug, dull, blunt,
Ringing the white china.
How they awaited him, those little deaths!
They waited like sweethearts. They excited him.

And we, too, had a relationship---
Tight wires between us,
Pegs too deep to uproot, and a mind like a ring
Sliding shut on some quick thing,
The constriction killing me also.

Thalidomide

O half moon---

Half-brain, luminosity---
Negro, masked like a white,

Your dark
Amputations crawl and appall---

Spidery, unsafe.
What glove

What leatheriness
Has protected

Me from that shadow---
The indelible buds,

Knuckles at shoulder-blades, the
Faces that

Shove into being, dragging
The lopped

Blood-caul of absences.
All night I carpenter

A space for the thing I am given,
A love

Of two wet eyes and a screech.
White spit

Of indifference!
The dark fruits revolve and fall.

The glass cracks across,
The image

Flees and aborts like dropped mercury.

The Applicant

First, are you our sort of person?
Do you wear
A glass eye, false teeth or a crutch,
A brace or a hook,
Rubber breasts or a rubber crotch,

Stitches to show something's missing? No, no? Then
How can we give you a thing?
Stop crying.
Open your hand.
Empty? Empty. Here is a hand

To fill it and willing
To bring teacups and roll away headaches
And do whatever you tell it.
Will you marry it?
It is guaranteed

To thumb shut your eyes at the end
And dissolve of sorrow.
We make new stock from the salt.
I notice you are stark naked.
How about this suit---

Black and stiff, but not a bad fit.
Will you marry it?
It is waterproof, shatterproof, proof
Against fire and bombs through the roof.
Believe me, they'll bury you in it.

Now your head, excuse me, is empty.
I have the ticket for that.
Come here, sweetie, out of the closet.
Well, what do you think of <u>that</u>?
Naked as paper to start

The Applicant (2)

But in twenty-five years she'll be silver,
In fifty, gold.
A living doll, everywhere you look.
It can sew, it can cook,
It can talk, talk, talk.

It works, there is nothing wrong with it.
You have a hole, it's a poultice.
You have an eye, it's an image.
My boy, it's your last resort.
Will you marry it, marry it, marry it.

Barren Woman

Empty, I echo to the least footfall,
Museum without statues, grand with pillars, porticoes, rotundas.
In my courtyard a fountain leaps and sinks back into itself,
Nun-hearted and blind to the world. Marble lilies
Exhale their pallor like scent.

I imagine myself with a great public,
Mother of a white Nike and several bald-eyed Apollos.
Instead, the dead injure me with attentions, and nothing can happen.
The moon lays a hand on my forehead,
Blank-faced and mum as a nurse.

Lady Lazarus

I have done it again.
One year in every ten
I manage it---

A sort of walking miracle, my skin
Bright as a Nazi lampshade,
My right foot

A paperweight,
My face a featureless, fine
Jew linen.

Peel off the napkin
O my enemy.
Do I terrify?---

The nose, the eye pits, the full set of teeth?
The sour breath
Will vanish in a day.

Soon, soon the flesh
The grave cave ate will be
At home on me

And I a smiling woman.
I am only thirty.
And like the cat I have nine times to die.

This is Number Three.
What a trash
To annihilate each decade.

Lady Lazarus (2)

What a million filaments.
The peanut-crunching crowd
Shoves in to see

Them unwrap me hand and foot---
The big strip tease.
Gentlemen, ladies

These are my hands
My knees.
I may be skin and bone,

Nevertheless, I am the same, identical woman.
The first time it happened I was ten.
It was an accident.

The second time I meant
To last it out and not come back at all.
I rocked shut

As a seashell.
They had to call and call
And pick the worms off me like sticky pearls.

Dying
Is an art, like everything else.
I do it exceptionally well.

I do it so it feels like hell.
I do it so it feels real.
I guess you could say I've a call.

It's easy enough to do it in a cell.
It's easy enough to do it and stay put.
It's the theatrical

Lady Lazarus (3)

Comeback in broad day   .
To the same place, the same face, the same brute
Amused shout:

'A miracle!'
That knocks me out.
There is a charge

For the eyeing of my scars, there is a charge
For the hearing of my heart---
It really goes!

And there is a charge, a very large charge
For a word or a touch
Or a bit of blood

Or a piece of my hair or my clothes!
So, so, Herr Doktor!
So, Herr Enemy.

I am your opus,
I am your valuable,
The pure gold baby

That melts to a shriek.
I turn and burn.
Do not think I underestimate your great concern!

Ash, ash/—
You poke and stir.
Flesh, bone, there is nothing there/---

A cake of soap,
A wedding ring,
A gold filling.

Lady Lazarus (4)

Herr God, Herr Lucifer
Beware
Beware.

Out of the ash
I rise with my red hair
And I eat men like air.

Tulips

The tulips are too excitable, it is winter here.
Look how white everything is, how quiet, how snowed-in.
I am learning peacefulness, lying by myself quietly
As the light lies on these white walls, this bed, these hands.
I am nobody; I have nothing to do with explosions.
I have given my name and my day-clothes up to the nurses
And my history to the anesthetist and my body to surgeons.

They have propped my head between the pillow and the sheet-cuff
Like an eye between two white lids that will not shut.
Stupid pupil, it has to take everything in.
The nurses pass and pass, they are no trouble,
They pass the way gulls pass inland in their white caps,
Doing things with their hands, one just the same as another,
So it is impossible to tell how many there are.

My body is a pebble to them, they tend it as water
Tends to the pebbles it must run over, smoothing them gently.
They bring me numbness in their bright needles, they bring me sleep.
Now I have lost myself I am sick of baggage---
My patent leather overnight case like a black pillbox,
My husband and child smiling out of the family photo;
Their smiles catch onto my skin, little smiling hooks.

I have let things slip, a thirty-year-old cargo boat
Stubbornly hanging on to my name and address.
They have swabbed me clear of my loving associations.
Scared and bare on the green plastic-pillowed trolley
I watched my teaset, my bureaus of linen, my books
Sink out of sight, and the water went over my head.
I am a nun now, I have never been so pure.

(next page)

Tulips (2)

I didn't want any flowers, I only wanted
To lie with my hands turned up and be utterly empty.
How free it is, you have no idea how free---
The peacefulness is so big it dazes you,
And it asks nothing, a name tag, a few trinkets.
It is what the dead close on, finally; I imagine them
Shutting their mouths on it, like a Communion tablet.

The tulips are too red in the first place, they hurt me.
Even through the gift paper I could hear them breathe
Lightly, through their white swaddlings, like an awful baby.
Their redness talks to my wound, it corresponds.
They are subtle: they seem to float, though they weigh me down,
Upsetting me with their sudden tongues and their color,
A dozen red lead sinkers round my neck.

Nobody watched me before, now I am watched.
The tulips turn to me, and the window behind me
Where once a day the light slowly widens and slowly thins,
And I see myself, flat, ridiculous, a cut-paper shadow
Between the eye of the sun and the eyes of the tulips,
And I have no face, I have wanted to efface myself.
The vivid tulips eat my oxygen.

Before they came the air was calm enough,
Coming and going, breath by breath, without any fuss.
Then the tulips filled it up like a loud noise.
Now the air snags and eddies round them the way a river
Snags and eddies round a sunken rust-red engine.
They concentrate my attention, that was happy
Playing and resting without committing itself.

The walls, also, seem to be warming themselves.
The tulips should be behind bars like dangerous animals;
They are opening like the mouth of some great African cat,
And I am aware of my heart: it opens and closes
Its bowl of red blooms out of sheer love of me.
The water I taste is warm and salt, like the sea,
And comes from a country far away as health.

A Secret

A secret! A secret!
How superior.
You are blue and huge, a traffic policeman,
Holding up one palm---

A difference between us?
I have one eye, you have two.
The secret is stamped on you,
Faint, undulant watermark.

Will it show in the black detector?
Will it come out
Wavery, indelible, true
Through the African giraffe in its Edeny greenery,

The Moroccan hippopotamus?
They stare from a square, stiff frill.
They are for export,
One a fool, the other a fool.

A secret. An extra amber
Brandy finger
Roosting and cooing 'You, you'
Behind two eyes in which nothing is reflected but monkeys.

A knife that can be taken out
To pare nails,
To lever the dirt.
'It won't hurt.'

An illegitimate baby--
That big blue head.
How it breathes in the bureau drawer.
'Is that lingerie, pet?

A Secret (2)

'It smells of salt cod, you had better
Stab a few cloves in an apple,
Make a sachet or
Do away with the bastard.

Do away with it altogether.'
'No, no, it is happy there.'
'But it wants to get out!
Look, look! It is wanting to crawl.'

My god, there goes the stopper!
The cars in the Place de la Concorde---
Watch out!
A stampede, a stampede—

Horns twirling, and jungle gutterals.
An exploded bottle of stout,
Slack foam in the lap.
You stumble out,

Dwarf baby,
The knife in your back.
'I feel weak.'
The secret is out.

The Jailor

My night sweats grease his breakfast plate.
The same placard of blue fog is wheeled into position
With the same trees and headstones.
Is that all he can come up with,
The rattler of keys?

I have been drugged and raped.
Seven hours knocked out of my right mind
Into a black sack
Where I relax, foetus or cat,
Lever of his wet dreams.

Something is gone.
My sleeping capsule, my red and blue zeppelin
Drops me from a terrible altitude.
Carapace smashed,
I spread to the beaks of birds.

O little gimlets———
What holes this papery day is already full of!
He has been burning me with cigarettes,
Pretending I am a negress with pink paws.
I am myself. That is not enough.

The fever trickles and stiffens in my hair.
My ribs show. What have I eaten?
Lies and smiles.
Surely the sky is not that color,
Surely the grass should be rippling.

All day, gluing my church of burnt matchsticks,
I dream of someone else entirely.

The Jailor (2)

And he, for this subversion
Hurts me, he
With his armory of fakery,

His high, cold masks of amnesia.
How did I get here?
Indeterminate criminal,
I die with variety---
Hung, starved, burned, hooked.

I imagine him
Impotent as distant thunder,
In whose shadow I have eaten my ghost ration.
I wish him dead or away.
That, it seems, is the impossibility.

That being free. What would the dark
Do without fevers to eat?
What would the light
Do without eyes to knife, what would he
Do, do, do without me.

Cut

for Susan O'Neill Roe

What a thrill—
My thumb instead of an onion.
The top quite gone
Except for a sort of a hinge

Of skin,
A flap like a hat,
Dead white.
Then that red plush.

Little pilgrim,
The Indian's axed your scalp.
Your turkey wattle
Carpet rolls

Straight from the heart.
I step on it,
Clutching my bottle
Of pink fizz.

A celebration, this is.
Out of a gap
A million soldiers run,
Redcoats, every one.

Whose side are they on?
O my
Homunculus, I am ill.
I have taken a pill to kill

The thin
Papery feeling.
Saboteur,
Kamikaze man---

Cut (2)

The stain on your
Gauze Ku Klux Klan
Babushka
Darkens and tarnishes and when

The balled
Pulp of your heart
Confronts its small
Mill of silence

How you jump---
Trepanned veteran,
Dirty girl,
Thumb stump?

Elm

(for Ruth Fainlight)

I know the bottom, she says. I know it with my great tap root:
It is what you fear.
I do not fear it: I have been there.

Is it the sea you hear in me,
Its dissatisfactions?
Or the voice of nothing, that was your madness?

Love is a shadow.
How you lie and cry after it
Listen: these are its hooves: it has gone off, like a horse.

All night I shall gallop thus, impetuously,
Till your head is a stone, your pillow a little turf,
Echoing, echoing.

Or shall I bring you the sound of poisons?
This is rain now, this big hush.
And this is the fruit of it: tin-white, like arsenic.

I have suffered the atrocity of sunsets.
Scorched to the root
My red filaments burn and stand, a hand of wires.

Now I break up in pieces that fly about like clubs.
A wind of such violence
Will tolerate no bystanding: I must shriek.

The moon, also, is merciless: she would drag me
Cruelly, being barren.
Her radiance scathes me. Or perhaps I have caught her.

(next page)

Elm (2)

I let her go. I let her go
Diminished and flat, as after radical surgery.
How your bad dreams possess and endow me!

I am inhabited by a cry.
Nightly it flaps out
Looking, with its hooks, for something to love.

I am terrified by this dark thing
That sleeps in me;
All day I feel its soft, feathery turnings, its malignity.

Clouds pass and disperse.
Are those the faces of love, those pale irretrievables?
Is it for such I agitate my heart?

I am incapable of more knowledge.
What is this, this face
So murderous in its strangle of branches?---

Its snaky acids hiss.
It petrifies the will. These are the isolate, slow faults
That kill, that kill, that kill.

The Night Dances

A smile fell in the grass.
Irretrievable!

And how will your night dances
Lose themselves. In mathematics?

Such pure leaps and spirals---
Surely they travel

The world forever, I shall not entirely
Sit emptied of beauties, the gift

Of your small breath, the drenched grass
Smell of your sleeps, lilies, lilies.

Their flesh bears no relation.
Cold folds of ego, the calla,

And the tiger, embellishing itself---
Spots, and a spread of hot petals.

The comets
Have such a space to cross

Such coldness, forgetfulness.
So your gestures flake off---

Warm and human, then their pink light
Bleeding and peeling

Through the black amnesias of heaven.
Why am I given

The Night Dances (2)

These lamps, these planets
Falling like blessings, like flakes

Six-sided, white
On my eyes, my lips, my hair

Touching and melting.
Nowhere.

The Detective

What was she doing when it blew in
Over the seven hills, the red furrow, the blue mountain?
Was she arranging cups? It is important.
Was she at the window, listening?
In that valley the train shrieks echo like souls on hooks.

That is the valley of death, though the cows thrive.
In her garden the lies were shaking out their moist silks
And the eyes of the killer moving sluglike and sidelong,
Unable to face the fingers, those egotists.
The fingers were tamping a woman into a wall,

A body into a pipe, and the smoke rising.
This is the smell of years burning, here in the kitchen,
These are the deceits, tacked up like family photographs,
And this is a man, look at his smile,
The death weapon? No-one is dead.

There is no body in the house at all.
There is the smell of polish, there are plush carpets.
There is the sunlight, playing its blades,
Bored hoodlum in a red room
Where the wireless talks to itself like an elderly relative.

Did it come like an arrow, did it come like a knife?
Which of the poisons is it?
Which of the nerve-curlers, the convulsors? Did it electrify?
This is a case without a body.
The body does not come into it at all.

It is a case of vaporization.
The mouth first, its absence reported
In the second year. It had been insatiable

The Detective (2)

And in punishment was hung out like brown fruit
To wrinkle and dry.

The breasts next.
These were harder, two white stones.
The milk came yellow, then blue and sweet as water.
There was no absence of lips, there were two children,
But their bones showed, and the moon smiled.

Then the dry wood, the gates,
The brown motherly furrows, the whole estate.
We walk on air, Watson.
There is only the moon, embalmed in phosphorus.
There is only a crow in a tree. Make notes.

Ariel

Stasis in darkness.
Then the substanceless blue
Pour of tor and distances.

God's lioness,
How one we grow,
Pivot of heels and knees!—The furrow

Splits and passes, sister to
The brown arc
Of the neck I cannot catch,

Nigger-eye
Berries cast dark
Hooks---

Black sweet blood mouthfuls,
Shadows.
Something else

Hauls me through air---
Thighs, hair;
Flakes from my heels.

White
Godiva, I unpeel---
Dead hands, dead stringencies.

And now I
Foam to wheat, a glitter of seas.
The child's cry

Ariel (2)

Melts in the wall.
And I
Am the arrow,

The dew that flies
Suicidal, at one with the drive
Into the red

Eye, the cauldron of morning.

Death & Co.

Two. Of course there are two.
It seems perfectly natural now---
The one who never looks up, whose eyes are lidded
And balled, like Blake's,
Who exhibits

The birthmarks that are his trademark---
The scald scar of water,
The nude
Verdigris of the condor.
I am red meat. His beak

Claps sidewise: I am not his yet.
He tells me how badly I photograph.
He tells me how sweet
The babies look in their hospital
Icebox, a simple

Frill at the neck,
Then the flutings of their Ionian
Death-gowns,
Then two little feet.
He does not smile or smoke.

The other does that,
His hair long and plausive.
Bastard
Masturbating a glitter,
He wants to be loved.

I do not stir.
The frost makes a flower,
The dew makes a star.
The dead bell,
The dead bell.

Somebody's done for.

Magi

The abstracts hover like dull angels:
Nothing so vulgar as a nose or an eye
Bossing the ethereal blanks of their face-ovals.

Their whiteness bears no relation to laundry,
Snow, chalk or suchlike. They're
The real thing, all right: the Good, the True---

Salutary and pure as boiled water,
Loveless as the multiplication table.
While the child smiles into thin air.

Six months in the world, and she is able
To rock on all fours like a padded hammock.
For her, the heavy notion of Evil

Attending her cot is less than a belly ache,
And Love the mother of milk, no theory.
They mistake their star, these papery godfolk.

They want the crib of some lamp-headed Plato.
Let them astound his heart with their merit.
What girl ever flourished in such company?

.

Lesbos

Viciousness in the kitchen!
The potatoes hiss.
It is all Hollywood, windowless,
The fluorescent light wincing on and off like a terrible migraine,
Coy paper strips for doors---
Stage curtains, a widow's frizz.
And I, love, am a pathological liar,
And my child---look at her, face down on the floor,
Little unstrung puppet, kicking to disappear---
Why she is a schizophrenic,
Her face red and white, a panic.
You have stuck her kittens outside your window
In a sort of cement well
Where they crap and puke and cry and she can't hear.
You say you can't stand her,
The bastard's a girl.
You who have blown your tubes like a bad radio
Clear of voices and history, the staticky
Noise of the new.
You say I should drown the kittens. Their smell!
You say I should drown my girl.
She'll cut her throat at ten if she's mad at two.
The baby smiles, fat snail,
From the polished lozenges of orange linoleum.
You could eat him. He's a boy.
You say your husband is just no good to you,
His Jew-mama guards his sweet sex like a pearl.
You have one baby, I have two.
I should sit on a rock off Cornwall and comb my hair.
I should wear tiger pants, I should have an affair.
We should meet in another life, we should meet in air,
Me and you.

Meanwhile there's a stink of fat and baby crap.
I'm doped and thick from my last sleeping pill.
The smog of cooking, the smog of hell
Floats our heads, two venomous opposites,
Our bones, our hair.
I call you Orphan, orphan. You are ill.
The sun gives you ulcers, the wind gives you t.b.
Once you were beautiful.
In New York, Hollywood, the men said: 'Through?
Gee baby, you are rare.'
You acted, acted, acted for the thrill.
The impotent husband slumps out for a coffee.
I try to keep him in,
An old pole for the lightning,
The acid baths, the skyfuls off of you.
He lumps it down the plastic cobbled hill,
Flogged trolley. The sparks are blue.
The blue sparks spill,
Splitting like quartz into a million bits.

O jewel! O valuable!
That night the moon
Dragged its blood bag, sick
Animal
Up over the harbor lights.
And then grew normal,
Hard and apart and white.
The scale-sheen on the sand scared me to death.
We kept picking up handfuls, loving it,
Working it like dough, a mulatto body,
The silk grits.
A dog picked up your doggy husband. They went on.

Now I am silent, hate
Up to my neck,
Thick, thick!

Lesbos (3)

I do not speak.
I am packing the hard potatoes like good clothes,
I am packing the babies,
I am packing the sick cats.
O vase of acid,
It is love you are full of. You know who you hate.
He is hugging his ball and chain down by the gate
That opens to the sea
Where it drives in, white and black,
Then spews it back.
Every day you fill him with soul-stuff, like a pitcher.
You are so exhausted.
Your voice my ear-ring,
Flapping and sucking, blood-loving bat.
That is that. That is that.
You peer from the door,
Sad hag. 'Every woman's a whore.
I can't communicate.'

I see your cute décor
Close on you like the fist of a baby
Or an anemone, that sea
Sweetheart, that kleptomaniac.
I am still raw.
I say I may be back.
You know what lies are for.

Even in your Zen heaven we shan't meet.

The Other

You come in late, wiping your lips.
What did I leave untouched on the doorstep---

White Nike,
Streaming between my walls?

Smilingly, blue lightning
Assumes, like a meathook, the burden of his parts.

The police love you, you confess everything.
Bright hair, shoe-black, old plastic,

Is my life so intriguing?
Is it for this you widen your eye-rings?

Is it for this the air motes depart?
They are not air motes, they are corpuscles.

Open your handbag. What is that bad smell?
It is your knitting, busily

Hooking itself to itself,
It is your sticky candies.

I have your head on my wall.
Navel cords, blue-red and lucent,

Shriek from my belly like arrows, and these I ride.
O moon-glow, o sick one,

The stolen horses, the fornications
Circle a womb of marble.

(next page)

The Other (2)

Where are you going
That you suck breath like mileage?

Sulphurous adulteries grieve in a dream.
Cold glass, how you insert yourself

Between myself and myself.
I scratch like a cat.

The blood that runs is dark fruit---
An effect, a cosmetic.

You smile.
No, it is not fatal.

Stopped Dead

A squeal of brakes.
Or is it a birth cry?
And here we are, hung out over the dead drop
Uncle, pants factory Fatso, millionaire?
And you out cold beside me in your chair.

The wheels, two rubber grubs, bite their sweet tails.
Is that Spain down there?
Red and yellow, two passionate hot metals
Writhing and sighing, what sort of a scenery is it?
It isn't England, it isn't France, it isn't Ireland.

It's violent. We're here on a visit,
With a goddam baby screaming off somewhere.
There's always a bloody baby in the air.
I'd call it a sunset, but
Whoever heard a sunset yowl like that?

You are sunk in your seven chins, still as a ham.
Who do you think I am,
Uncle, uncle?
Sad Hamlet, with a knife?
Where do you stash your life?

Is it a penny, a pearl---
Your soul, your soul?
I'll carry it off like a rich pretty girl,
Simply open the door and step out of the car
And live in Gibraltar on air, on air.

Poppies in October

for Helder & Suzetta Macedo

Even the sun-clouds this morning cannot manage such skirts.
Nor the woman in the ambulance
Whose red heart blooms through her coat so astoundingly---

A gift, a love gift
Utterly unasked for
By a sky

Palely and flamily
Igniting its carbon monoxides, by eyes
Dulled to a halt under bowlers.

O my God, what am I
That these late mouths should cry open
In a forest of frost, in a dawn of cornflowers.

The Courage of ~~Quietness~~ Shutting-Up

The courage of the shut mouth, in spite of artillery!
The line pink and quiet, a worm, basking.
There are black discs behind it, the discs of outrage,
And the outrage of a sky, the lined brain of it.
The discs revolve, they ask to be heard,

Loaded, as they are, with accounts of bastardies.
Bastardies, usages, desertions and doubleness,
The needle journeying in its groove,
Silver beast between two dark canyons,
A great surgeon, now a tattooist,

Tattooing over and over the same blue grievances,
The snakes, the babies, the tits
On mermaids and two-legged dreamgirls.
The surgeon is quiet, he does not speak.
He has seen too much death, his hands are full of it.

So the discs of the brain revolve, like the muzzles of cannon.
Then there is that antique billhook, the tongue,
Indefatigable, purple. Must it be cut out?
It has nine tails, it is dangerous.
And the noise it flays from the air, once it gets going!

No, the tongue, too, has been put by
Hung up in the library with the engravings of Rangoon
And the fox heads, the otter heads, the heads of dead rabbits.
It is a marvellous object —
The things it has pierced in its time!

But how about the eyes, the eyes, the eyes?
Mirrors can kill and talk, they are terrible rooms
In which a torture goes on one can only watch.

The Courage of Quietness (2)

The face that lived in this mirror is the face of a dead man.
Do not worry about the eyes---

They may be white and shy, they are no stool pigeons,
Their death rays folded like flags

Of a country no longer heard of,
An obstinate independency
Insolvent among the mountains.

Nick and the Candlestick

I am a miner. The light burns blue.
Waxy stalacmites
Drip and thicken, tears

The earthen womb
Exudes from its dead boredom.
Black bat airs

Wrap me, raggy shawls,
Cold homicides.
They weld to me like plums.

Old cave of calcium
Icicles, old echoer
Even the newts are white,

Those holy Joes.
And the fish, the fish---
Christ! they are panes of ice,

A vice of knives,
A piranha
Religion, drinking

Its first communion out of my live toes.
The candle
Gulps and recovers its small altitude,

Its yellows hearten.
O love, how did you get here?
O embryo

Remembering, even in sleep,
Your crossed position.
The blood blooms clean

Nick and the Candlestick (2)

In you, ruby.
The pain
You wake to is not yours.

Love, love,
I have hung our cave with roses,
With soft rugs---

The last of Victoriana.
Let the stars
Plummet to their dark address,

Let the mercuric
Atoms that cripple drip
Into the terrible well,

You are the one
Solid the spaces lean on, envious.
You are the baby in the barn.

Berck-Plage

1.
This is the sea, then, this great abeyance.
How the sun's poultice draws on my inflamation!

Electrifyingly-colored sherbets, scooped from the freeze
By pale girls, travel the air in scorched hands.

Why is it so quiet, what are they hiding?
I have two legs, and I move smilingly.

A sandy damper kills the vibrations;
It stretches for miles, the shrunk voices

Waving and crutchless, half their old size.
The lines of the eye, scalded by these bald surfaces,

Boomerang like anchored elastics, hurting the owner.
Is it any wonder he puts on dark glasses?

Is it any wonder he affects a black cassock?
Here he comes now, among the mackerel gatherers

Who wall up their backs against him.
They are handling the black and green lozenges like the parts of a body.

The sea, that crystallized these,
Creeps away, many-snaked, with a long hiss of distress.

2.
This black boot has no mercy for anybody.
Why should it, it is the hearse of a dead foot,

The high, dead, toeless foot of this priest
Who plumbs the well of his book,

(next page)

Berck-Plage (2)

The bent print bulging before him like scenery.
Obscene bikinis hide in the dunes,

Breasts and hips a confectioner's sugar
Of little crystals, titillating the light,

While a green pool opens its eye,
Sick with what it has swallowed---

Limbs, images, shrieks. Behind the concrete bunkers
Two lovers unstick themselves.

O white sea-crockery,
What cupped sighs, what salt in the throat!

And the onlooker, trembling,
Drawn like a long material

Through a still virulence,
And a weed, hairy as privates.

3.
On the balconies of the hotel, things are glittering.
Things, things---

Tubular steel wheelchairs, aluminum crutches!
Such salt-sweetness! Why should I walk

Beyond the breakwater, spotty with barnacles?
I am not a nurse, white and attendant,

I am not a smile.
These children are after something, with hooks and cries,

And my heart too small to bandage their terrible faults.
This is the side of a man: his red ribs,

(next page)

Berck-Plage (3)

The nerves bursting like trees, and this is the surgeon:
One mirrory eye---

A facet of knowledge.
On a striped mattress in one room

An old man is vanishing.
There is no help in his weeping wife.

Where are the eye-stones, yellow and valuable,
And the tongue, sapphire of ash.

4.
A wedding-cake face in a paper frill.
How superior he is now.

It is like possessing a saint.
The nurses in their wing-caps are no longer so beautiful;

They are browning, like touched gardenias.
The bed is rolled from the wall.

This is what it is to be complete. It is horrible.
Is he wearing pajamas or an evening suit

Under the glued sheet from which his powdery beak
Rises so whitely, unbuffeted?

They propped his jaw with a book until it stiffened
And folded his hands, that were shaking: goodbye, goodbye.

Now the washed sheets fly in the sun,
The pillow cases are sweetening.

It is a blessing, it is a blessing:
The long coffin of soap-colored oak,

The curious bearers and the raw date
Engraving itself in silver with marvelous calm.

5.
The grey sky lowers, the hills like a green sea
Run fold upon fold far off, concealing their hollows,

The hollows in which rock the thoughts of the wife---
Blunt, practical boats

Full of dresses and hats and china and married daughters.
In the parlor of the stone house

One curtain is flickering from the open window,
Flickering and pouring, a pitiful candle.

This is the tongue of the dead man: remember, remember.
How far he is now, his actions

Around him like livingroom furniture, like a décor.
As the pallors gather---

The pallors of hands and neighborly faces,
The elate pallors of flying iris.

They are flying off into nothing: remember us.
The empty benches of memory look over stones,

Marble façades with blue veins, and jelly-glassfuls of daffodils.
It is so beautiful up here: it is a stopping place.

6.
The unnatural fatness of these lime leaves!---
Pollarded green balls, the trees march to church.

The voice of the priest, in thin air,
Meets the corpse at the gate,

Addressing it, while the hills roll the notes of the dead bell;
A glitter of wheat and crude earth.

What is the name of that color?---
Old blood of caked walls the sun heals,

Old blood of limb stumps, burnt hearts.
The widow with her black pocketbook and three daughters,

Necessary among the flowers,
Enfolds her face like fine linen,

Not to be spread again.
While a sky, wormy with put-by smiles,

Passes cloud after cloud.
And the bride flowers expend a freshness,

And the soul is a bride
In a still place, and the groom is red and forgetful, he is featureless.

7.
Behind the glass of this car
The world purrs, shut-off and gentle.

And I am dark-suited and still, a member of the party,
Gliding up in low gear behind the cart.

And the priest is a vessel,
A tarred fabric, sorry and dull,

Following the coffin on its flowery cart like a beautiful woman,
A crest of breasts, eyelids and lips

Storming the hilltop.
Then, from the barred yard, the children

Smell the melt of shoe-blacking,
Their faces turning, wordless and slow,

(next page)

Berck-Plage (6)

Their eyes opening
On a wonderful thing---

Six round black hats in the grass and a lozenge of wood,
And a naked mouth, red and awkward.

For a minute the sky pours into the hole like plasma.
There is no hope, it is given up.

.   .   .   .   .   .

Gulliver

Over your body the clouds go
High, high and icily
And a little flat, as if they

Floated on a glass that was invisible.
Unlike swans,
Having no reflections;

Unlike you,
With no strings attached.
All cool, all blue. Unlike you---

You, there on your back,
Eyes to the sky.
The spider-men have caught you,

Winding and twining their petty fetters,
Their bribes---
So many silks.

How they hate you.
They converse in the valley of your fingers, they are inchworms.
They would have you sleep in their cabinets,

This toe and that toe, a relic.
Step off!
Step off seven leagues, like those distances

That revolve in Crivelli, untouchable.
Let this eye be an eagle,
The shadow of this lip, an abyss.

Getting There

How far is it?
How far is it now?
The gigantic gorilla interior
Of the wheels move, they appal me---
The terrible brains
Of Krupp, black muzzles
Revolving, the sound
Punching out Absence! like cannon.
It is Russia I have to get across, it is some war or other.
I am dragging my body
Quietly through the straw of the boxcars.
Now is the time for bribery.
What do wheels eat, these wheels
Fixed to their arcs like gods,
The silver leash of the will---
Inexorable. And their pride!
All the gods know is destinations.
I am a letter in this slot---
I fly to a name, two eyes.
Will there be fire, will there be bread?
Here there is such mud.
It is a trainstop, the nurses
Undergoing the faucet water, its veils, veils in a nunnery,
Touching their wounded,
The men the blood still pumps forward,
Legs, arms piled outside
The tent of unending cries.
A hospital of dolls.
And the men, what is left of the men
Pumped ahead by these pistons, this blood
Into the next mile,
The next hour---
Dynasty of broken arrows!

Getting There (2)

How far is it?
There is mud on my feet,
Thick, red and slipping. It is Adam's side,
This earth I rise from, and I in agony.
I cannot undo myself, and the train is steaming.
Steaming and breathing, its teeth
Ready to roll, like a devil's.
There is a minute at the end of it
A minute, a dewdrop.
How far is it?
It is so small
The place I am getting to, why are there these obstacles---
The body of this ~~beautiful~~ woman,
Charred skirts and deathmask
Mourned by religious figures, by garlanded children.
And now detonations—
Thunder and guns.
The fire's between us.
Is there no still place
Turning and turning in the middle air,
Untouched and untouchable.
The train is dragging itself, it is screaming---
(An)animal
Insane for the destination,
The bloodspot,
The face at the end of the flare.
I shall bury the wounded like pupas,
I shall count and bury the dead.
Let their souls writhe in a dew,
Incense in my track.
The carriages rock, they are cradles.
And I, stepping from this skin
Of old bandages, boredoms, old faces

Step to you from the black car of Lethe,
Pure as a baby.

Medusa

Off that landspit of stony mouth-plugs,
Eyes rolled by white sticks,
Ears cupping the sea's incoherences,
You house your unnerving head---God-ball,
Lens of mercies,

Your stooges
Plying their wild cells in my keel's shadow,
Pushing by like hearts,
Red stigmata at the very center,
Riding the rip tide to the nearest point of departure,

Dragging their Jesus hair.
Did I escape, I wonder?
My mind winds to you,
Old barnacled umbilicus, Atlantic cable,
Keeping itself, it seems, in a state of miraculous repair.

In any case, you are always there,
Tremulous breath at the end of my line,
Curve of water upleaping
To my water rod, dazzling and grateful,
Touching and sucking.

I didn't call you.
I didn't call you at all.
Nevertheless, nevertheless
You steamed to me over the sea,
Fat and red, a placenta

Paralyzing the kicking lovers.
Cobra light
Squeezing the breath from the blood bells

Medusa (2)

Of the fuchsia. I could draw no breath,
Dead and moneyless,

Overexposed, like an X ray.
Who do you think you are?
A Communion wafer? Blubbery Mary?
I shall take no bite of your body,
Bottle in which I live,

Ghastly Vatican.
I am sick to death of hot salt.
Green as eunuchs, your wishes
Hiss at my sins.
Off, off, eely tentacle!

There is nothing between us.

Purdah

Jade---
Stone of the side,
The agonized

Side of a green Adam, I
Smile, cross-legged,
Enigmatical,

Shifting my clarities.
So valuable!
How the sun polishes this shoulder!

And should
The moon, my
Indefatigable cousin

Rise, with her cancerous pallors,
Dragging trees---
Little bushy polyps,

Little nets,
My visibilities hide.
I gleam like a mirror.

At this facet the bridegroom arrives,
Lord of the mirrors!
It is himself he guides

In among these silk
Screens, these rustling appurtenances.
I breathe, and the mouth

Veil stirs its curtain.
My eye
Veil is

Purdah (2)

A concatenation of rainbows.
I am his.
Even in his

Absence, I
Revolve in my
Sheath of impossibles,

Priceless and quiet
Among these parakeets, macaws!
O chatterers

Attendants of the eyelash!
I shall unloose
One feather, like the peacock.

Attendants of the lip!
I shall unloose
One note

Shattering
The chandelier
Of air that all day plies

Its crystals,
A million ignorants.
Attendants!

Attendants!
And at his next step
I shall unloose

I shall unloose——
From the small jeweled
Doll he guards like a heart———

The lioness,
The shriek in the bath,
The cloak of holes.

The Moon and the Yew Tree

This is the light of the mind, cold and planetary.
The trees of the mind are black. The light is blue.
The grasses unload their griefs on my feet as if I were God,
Prickling my ankles and murmuring of their humility.
Fumey, spiritous mists inhabit this place
Separated from my house by a row of headstones.
I simply cannot see where there is to get to.

The moon is no door. It is a face in its own right,
White as a knuckle and terribly upset.
It drags the sea after it like a dark crime; it is quiet
With the O-gape of complete despair. I live here.
Twice on Sunday, the bells startle the sky---
Eight great tongues affirming the Resurrection.
At the end, they soberly bong out their names.

The yew tree points up. It has a Gothic shape.
The eyes lift after it and find the moon.
The moon is my mother. She is not sweet like Mary.
Her blue garments unloose small bats and owls.
How I would like to believe in tenderness|---
The face of the effigy, gentled by candles,
Bending, on me in particular, its mild eyes.

I have fallen a long way. Clouds are flowering
Blue and mystical over the face of the stars.
Inside the church, the saints will be all blue,
Floating on their delicate feet over the cold pews,
Their hands and faces stiff with holiness.
The moon sees nothing of this. She is bald and wild.
And the message of the yew tree is blackness---blackness and silence.

A Birthday Present

What is this, behind this veil, is it ugly, is it beautiful?
It is shimmering, has it breasts, has it edges?

I am sure it is unique, I am sure it is just what I want.
When I am quiet at my cooking I feel it looking, I feel it thinking

'Is this the one I am to appear for,
Is this the elect one, the one with black eye-pits and a scar?

Measuring the flour, cutting off the surplus,
Adhering to rules, to rules, to rules.

Is this the one for the annunciation?
My god, what a laugh!'

But it shimmers, it does not stop, and I think it wants me.
I would not mind if it was bones, or a pearl button.

I do not want much of a present, anyway, this year.
After all, I am alive only by accident.

I would have killed myself gladly that time any possible way.
Now there are these veils, shimmering like curtains,

The diaphanous satins of a January window
White as babies' bedding and glittering with dead breath. O ivory!

It must be a tusk there, a ghost-column.
Can you not see I do not mind what it is

Can you not give it to me?
Do not be ashamed---I do not mind if it is small.

A Birthday Present (2)

Do not be mean, I am ready for enormity.
Let us sit down to it, one on either side, admiring the gleam,

The glaze, the mirrory variety of it.
Let us eat our last supper at it, like a hospital plate.

I know why you will not give it to me,
You are terrified

The world will go up in a shriek, and your head with it,
Bossed, brazen, an antique shield,

A marvel to your great-grandchildren.
Do not be afraid, it is not so.

I will only take it and go aside quietly.
You will not even hear me opening it, no paper crackle,

No falling ribbons, no scream at the end.
I do not think you credit me with this discretion.

If you only knew how the veils were killing my days!
To you they are only transparencies, clear air,

But my god, the clouds are like cotton.
Armies of them! They are carbon monoxide.

Sweetly, sweetly I breathe in,
Filling my veins with invisibles, with the million

Probably motes that tick the years off my life.
You are silver-suited for the occasion. O adding machine

Is it impossible for you to let something go and have it go whole?
Must you stamp each piece in purple,

A Birthday Present (3)

Must you kill what you can?
There is this one thing I want today, and only you can give it to me.

It stands at my window, big as the sky.
It breathes from my sheets, the cold, dead center

Where spilt lives congeal and stiffen to history.
Let it not come by the mail, finger by finger.

Let it not come by word of mouth, I should be sixty
By the time the whole of it was delivered, and too numb to use it.

Only let down the veil, the veil, the veil.
If it were death

I would admire the deep gravity of it, its timeless eyes.
I would know you were serious.

There would be a nobility then, there would be a birthday.
And the knife not carve, but enter

Pure and clean as the cry of a baby,
And the universe slide from my side.

Letter in November

Love, the world
Suddenly turns, turns color. The streetlight
Splits through the rat's-tail
Pods of the laburnum at nine in the morning.
It is the Arctic,

This little black
Circle, with its tawn silk grasses---babies' hair.
There is a green in the air,
Soft, delectable.
It cushions me lovingly.

I am flushed and warm.
I think I may be enormous,
I am so stupidly happy,
My Wellingtons
Squelching and squelching through the beautiful red.

This is my property.
Two times a day
I pace it, sniffing
The barbarous holly with its viridian
Scallops, pure iron,

And the wall of old corpses.
I love them.
I love 6hem like history.
The apples are golden,
Imagine it---

My seventy trees
Holding their gold-ruddy balls
In a thick grey death-soup,

Letter in November (2)

Their million
Gold leaves metal and breathless.

O love, O celibate.
Nobody but me
Walks the waist-high wet.
The irreplaceable
Golds bleed and deepen, the mouths of Thermopylae.

Amnesiac

No use, no use, now, begging Recognize.
There is nothing to do with such a beautiful blank but smooth it.
Name, house, car keys,

The little toy wife
Erased, sigh, sigh.
Four babies and a cocker.

Nurses the size of worms and a minute doctor
Tuck him in.
Old happenings

Peel from his skin.
Down the drain with all of it!
Hugging his pillow

Like the red-headed sister he never dared to touch,
He dreams of a new one---
Barren, the lot are barren.

And of another color.
How they'll travel, travel, travel, scenery
Sparking off their brother-sister rears,

A comet tail.
And money the sperm fluid of it all.
One nurse brings in

A green drink, one a blue.
They rise on either side of him like stars.
The two drinks flame and foam.

O sister, mother, wife,
Sweet Lethe is my life.
I am never, never, never coming home!

The Rival

If the moon smiled, she would resemble you.
You leave the same impression
Of something beautiful, but annihilating.
Both of you are great light borrowers.
Her O-mouth grieves at the world; yours is unaffected,

And your first gift is making stone out of everything.
I wake to a mausoleum; you are here,
Ticking your fingers on the marble table, looking for cigarettes,
Spiteful as a woman, but not so nervous,
And dying to say something unanswerable.

The moon, too, abases her subjects,
But in the daytime she is ridiculous.
Your dissatisfactions, on the other hand,
Arrive through the mailslot with loving regularity,
White and blank, expansive as carbon monoxide.

No day is safe from news of you,
Walking about in Africa maybe, but thinking of me.

Daddy

You do not do, you do not do
Any more, black shoe
In which I have lived like a foot
For thirty years, poor and white,
Barely daring to breathe or Achoo.

Daddy, I have had to kill you.
You died before I had time---
Marble-heavy, a bag full of God,
Ghastly statue with one grey toe
Big as a Frisco seal

And a head in the freakish Atlantic
Where it pours bean green over blue
In the waters off beautiful Nauset.
I used to pray to recover you.
Ach, du.

In the German tongue, in the Polish town
Scraped flat by the roller
Of wars, wars, wars.
But the name of the town is common.
My Polack friend

Says there are a dozen or two.
So I never could tell where you
Put your foot, your root,
I never could talk to you.
The tongue stuck in my jaw.

It stuck in a barb wire snare.
Ich, ich, ich, ich,
I could hardly speak.
I thought every German was you.
And the language obscene

An engine, an engine
Chuffing me off like a Jew.
A Jew to Dachau, Auschwitz, Belsen.
I began to talk like a Jew.
I think I may well be a Jew.

The snows of the Tyrol, the clear beer of Vienna
Are not very pure or true.
With my gypsy ancestress and my weird luck
And my Taroc pack and my Taroc pack
I may be a bit of a Jew.

I have always been scared of you,
With your Luftwaffe, your gobbledygoo.
And your neat moustache
And your Aryan eye, bright blue.
Panzer-man, panzer-man, o You——

Not God but a swastika
So black no sky could squeak through.
Every woman adores a Fascist,
The boot in the face, the brute
Brute heart of a brute like you.

You stand at the blackboard, daddy,
In the picture I have of you,
A cleft in your chin instead of your foot
But no less a devil for that, no not
Any less the black man who

Bit my pretty red heart in two.
I was ten when they buried you.
At twenty I tried to die
And get back, back, back to you.
I thought even the bones would do.

Daddy (3)

But they pulled me out of the sack,
And they stuck me together with glue.
And then I knew what to do.
I made a model of you,
A man in black with a Meinkampf look

And a love of the rack and the screw.
And I said I do, I do.
So daddy, I'm finally through.
The black telephone's off at the root,
The voices just can't worm through.

If I've killed one man, I've killed two---
The vampire who said he was you
And drank my blood for a year,
Seven years, if you want to know.
Daddy, you can lie back now.

There's a stake in your fat black heart
And the villagers never liked you.
They are dancing and stamping on you.
They always <u>knew</u> it was you.
Daddy, daddy, you bastard, I'm through.

You're

Clownlike, happiest on your hands,
Feet to the stars, and moon-skulled,
Gilled like a fish. A common-sense
Thumbs-down on the dodo's mode.
Wrapped up in yourself like a spool,
Trawling your dark as owls do.
Mute as a turnip from the Fourth
Of July to All Fools' Day,
O high-riser, my little loaf.

Vague as fog and looked for like mail.
Farther off than Australia.
Bent-backed Atlas, our traveled prawn.
Snug as a bud and at home
Like a sprat in a pickle jug.
A creel of eels, all ripples.
Jumpy as a Mexican bean.
Right, like a well-done sum.
A clean slate, with your own face on.

Fever 193°

Pure? What does it mean?
The tongues of hell
Are dull, dull as the triple

Tongues of dull, fat Cerberus
Who wheezes at the gate. Incapable
Of licking clean

The aguey tendon, the sin, the sin.
The tinder cries.
The indelible smell

Of a snuffed candle! .
Love, love, the low smokes roll
From me like Isadora's scarves, I'm in a fright

One scarf will catch and anchor in the wheel.
Such yellow sullen smokes
Make their own element. They will not rise,

But trundle round the globe
Choking the aged and the meek,
The weak

Hothouse baby in its crib,
The ghastly orchid
Hanging its hanging garden in the air,

Devilish leopard!
Radiation turned it white
And killed it in an hour.

Greasing the bodies of adulterers
Like Hiroshima ash and eating in.
The sin. The sin.

Fever 103° (2)

Darling, all night
I have been flickering, off, on, off, on.
The sheets grow heavy as a lecher's kiss.

Three days. Three nights.
Lemon water, chicken
Water, water make me retch.

I am too pure for you or anyone.
Your body
Hurts me as the world hurts God. I am a lantern---

My head a moon
Of Japanese paper, my gold beaten skin
Infinitely delicate and infinitely expensive.

Does not my heat astound you. And my light.
All by myself I am a huge camellia
Glowing and coming and going, flush on flush.

I think I am going up,
I think I may rise---
The beads of hot metal fly, and I, love, I

Am a pure acetylene
Virgin
Attended by roses,

By kisses, by cherubim,
By whatever these pink things mean.
Not you, nor him

Nor him, nor him
(My selves dissolving, old whore petticoats)---
To Paradise.

The Bee Meeting

Who are these people at the bridge to meet me? They are the villagers---
The rector, the midwife, the sexton, the agent for bees.
In my sleeveless summery dress I have no protection,
And they are all gloved and covered, why did nobody tell me?
They are smiling and taking out veils tacked to ancient hats.

I am nude as a chicken neck, does nobody love me?
Yes, here is the secretary of bees with her white shop smock,
Buttoning the cuffs at my wrists and the slit from my neck to my knees.
Now I am milkweed silk, the bees will not notice.
They will not smell my fear, my fear, my fear.

Which is the rector now, is it that man in black?
Which is the midwife, is that her blue coat?
Everybody is nodding a square black head, they are knights in visors,
Breastplates of cheesecloth knotted under the armpits.
Their smiles and their voices are changing. I am led through a beanfield,

Strips of tinfoil winking like people,
Feather dusters fanning their hands in a sea of bean flowers,
Creamy bean flowers with black eyes and leaves like bored hearts.
Is it blood clots the tendrils are dragging up that string?
No, no, it is scarlet flowers that will one day be edible.

Now they are giving me a fashionable white straw Italian hat
And a black veil that molds to my face, they are making me one of them.
They are leading me to the shorn grove, the circle of hives.
Is it the hawthorn that smells so sick?
The barren body of hawthorn, etherizing its children.

Is it some operation that is taking place?
It is the surgeon my neighbors are waiting for,

Bees (2)

This apparition in a green helmet,
Shining gloves and white suit.
Is it the butcher, the grocer, the postman, someone I know?

I cannot run, I am rooted, and the gorse hurts me
With its yellow purses, its spiky armory.
I could not run without having to run forever.
The white hive is snug as a virgin,
Sealing off her brood cells, her honey, and quietly humming.

Smoke rolls and scarves in the grove.
The mind of the hive thinks this is the end of everything.
Here they come, the outriders, on their hysterical elastics.
If I stand very still, they will think I am cow parsley,
A gullible head untouched by their animosity,

Not even nodding, a personage in a hedgerow.
The villagers open the chambers, they are hunting the queen.
Is she hiding, is she eating honey? She is very clever.
She is old, old, old, she must live another year, and she knows it.
While in their fingerjoint cells the new virgins

Dream of a duel they will win inevitably,
A curtain of wax dividing them from the bride flight,
The upflight of the murderess into a heaven that loves her.
The villagers are moving the virgins, there will be no killing.
The old queen does not show herself, is she so ungrateful?

I am exhausted, I am exhausted---
Pillar of white in a blackout of knives.
I am the magician's girl who does not flinch.
The villagers are untying their disguises, they are shaking hands.
Whose is that long white box in the grove, what have they accomplished,
    why am I cold?

The Arrival of the Bee Box

I ordered this, this clean wood box
Square as a chair and almost too heavy to lift.
I would say it was the coffin of a midget
Or a square baby
Were there not such a din in it.

The box is locked, it is dangerous.
I have to live with it overnight
And I can't keep away from it.
There are no windows, so I can't see what is in there.
There is only a little grid, no exit.

I put my eye to the grid.
It is dark, dark,
With the swarmy feeling of African hands
Minute and shrunk for export,
Black on black, angrily clambering.

How can I let them out.
It is the noise that appals me most of all,
The unintelligible syllables.
It is like a Roman mob,
Small, taken one by one, but my god, together!

I lay my ear to furious Latin.
I am not a Caesar.
I have simply ordered a box of maniacs.
They can be sent back.
They can die, I need feed them nothing, I am the owner.

I wonder how hungry they are.
I wonder if they would forget me
If I just undid the locks and stood back and turned into a tree.

Bees (4)

There is the laburnum, its blond colonnades,
And the petticoats of the cherry.

They might ignore me immediately
In my moon suit and funeral veil.
I am no source of honey
So why should they turn on me?
Tomorrow I will be sweet God, I will set them free.

The box is only temporary.

Stings

Bare-handed, I hand the combs.
The man in white smiles, bare-handed,
Our cheesecloth gauntlets neat and sweet,
The throats of our wrists brave lilies.
He and I

Have a thousand clean cells between us,
Eight combs of yellow cups,
And the hive itself a teacup,
White with pink flowers on it.
With excessive love I enameled it

Thinking 'Sweetness, sweetness.'
Brood cells grey as the fossils of shells
Terrify me, they seem so old.
What am I buying, wormy mahogany?
Is there any queen at all in it?

If there is, she is old,
Her wings torn shawls, her long body
Rubbed of its plush---
Poor and bare and unqueenly and even shameful.
I stand in a column

Of winged, unmiraculous women,
Honey-drudgers.
I am no drudge
Though for years I have eaten dust
And dried plates with my dense hair.

And seen my strangeness evaporate,
Blue dew from dangerous skin.
Will they hate me,

Stings (2)

These women who only scurry,
Whose news is the open cherry, the open clover?

It is almost over.
I am in control.
Here is my honey-machine,
It will work without thinking,
Opening, in spring, like an industrious virgin

To scour the creaming crests
As the moon, for its ivory powders, scours the sea.
A third person is watching.
He has nothing to do with the bee-seller or with me.
Now he is gone

In eight great bounds, a great scapegoat.
Here is his slipper, here is another,
And here the square of white linen
He wore instead of a hat.
He was sweet,

The sweat of his efforts a rain
Tugging the world to fruit.
The bees found him out,
Molding onto his lips like lies,
Complicating his features.

They thought death was worth it, but I
Have a self to recover, a queen.
Is she dead, is she sleeping?
Where has she been,
With her lion-red body, her wings of glass?

Now she is flying
More terrible than she ever was, red
Scar in the sky, red comet
Over the engine that killed her---
The mausoleum, the wax house.

Wintering

This is the easy time, there is nothing doing.
I have whirled the midwife's extractor,
I have my honey,
Six jars of it,
Six cat's eyes in the wine cellar,

Wintering in a dark without window
At the heart of the house
Next to the last tenant's rancid jam
And the bottles of empty glitters---
Sir So-and-so's gin.

This is the room I have never been in.
This is the room I could never breathe in.
The black bunched in there like a bat,
No light
But the torch and its faint

Chinee yellow on appalling objects---
Black asininity. Decay.
Possession.
It is they who own me.
Neither cruel nor indifferent,

Only ignorant.
This is the time of hanging on for the bees---the bees
So slow I hardly know them,
Filing like soldiers
To the syrup tin

To make up for the honey I've taken.
Tate and Lyle keeps them going,
The refined snow.

Wintering (2)

It is Tate and Lyle they live on, instead of flowers.
They take it. The cold sets in.

Now they ball in a mass,
Black
Mind against all that white.
The smile of the snow is white.
It spreads itself out, a mile-long body of Meissen,

Into which, on warm days,
They can only carry their dead.
The bees are all women,
Maids and the long royal lady.
They have got rid of the men,

The blunt, clumsy stumblers, the boors.
Winter is for women---
The woman, still at her knitting, ·
At the cradle of Spanish walnut,
Her body a bulb in the cold and too dumb to think.

Will the hive survive, will the gladiolas
Succeed in banking their fires
To enter another year?
What will they taste of, the Christmas roses?
The bees are flying. They taste the spring.

III

Facsimile drafts of the poem 'Ariel'

To give a sense of Sylvia Plath's creative process, here follow the working drafts in facsimile for the title poem 'Ariel.' The drafts are variously numbered and dated by Sylvia Plath. The first four drafts were written on the pink Smith College Memorandum paper, as were various other drafts of the *Ariel* poems. The poem 'Ariel' was accepted for publication by the *Observer* and was eventually published in the *Observer* on the third of November 1963, under a variant title, 'The Horse.' A typeset proof of the poem from the *Observer* is appended to the end of this section. It was corrected by Sylvia Plath in mid-December 1962.

ariel   cream dun   lioness of God
                                        dark bay
                                        bright bay

God's lioness also, how one we grow
Crude mover whom I move & bam to love
Pivot of heels & knees, and of my color.

Opens before ~~too~~ the red furrow,
~~The dull rump runs,~~ all soil substanceless
Stasis in darkness, then the blue
poureed of tor & distances.
God's lioness, how one we grow!

Pivot of heels & knees! the furrow
Splits & passes, sister to the brown arc
of the neck I cannot catch, nigger-eye

blackberries, multiplying cast ~~dark~~
~~stip~~
~~Hooks,~~ Hooks, but do not catch —
Black sweet blood mouthfuls! Something else

Hauls me through air// Flakes from my heels,
From white wheat, a glitter of seas,
I rise,

the arrow, the that flies
In the cauldron of morning
One white melt, upflung

to the lover, the plunging
Hooves I am, that over & over

Ariel

Stasis in darkness, then the substanceless blue
Pour of tor & distances.
God's lioness, how one we grow!

Pivot of heels & knees! The furrow
Splits & passes // sister to the brown arc
Of the neck I cannot catch // nigger-eye //

Berries, multiplying, cast dark
Hooks, but do not catch.
Black sweet blood mouthfuls!

Some thing else
Hauls me through air,
Flakes from my heels.

And now I.
Foam to bright wheat, a glitter of seas,

~~The fry~~
~~With the arrow, the dew that flies~~
The child's cry

Melts in the wall, and I
Am the arrow, the dew that flies
Suicidal, at one
With the drive
In to the red ~~eye~~ ~~heart~~; ~~into the cauldron~~
Eye, Into the cauldron of morning.

Ariel

③   October 27
        1962

Stasis in darkness,
Then the substanceless blue
Pour of tor & distances.

God's lioness!
How one we grow!
Pivot of heels & knees! The furrow

Splits & passes
Sister to the brown arc
Of the neck I cannot catch,

Nigger-eye
Berries cast dark
Hooks, ~~but~~ ~~do~~ ~~not~~ ~~stick~~ ~~black~~

~~Black~~ ~~black~~ sweet blood mouthfuls!
Shadows!
Something else

Hauls me through air—
Thighs, hair;
Flakes from my heels.   white
                              bodies, I unpeel—
                              Dead hands, dead
And now I   stringencies!
~~Foam~~ Foaming to wheat, a glitter of seas.
The child's cry

Melts in the wall.
O bright beast. I
Am the arrow, The dew that flies
Suicidal, at one with the drive
Into the red
Eye, the cauldron of morning.

~~Hands, hearts, dead men~~
~~Dead men~~
Hands, ~~hearts,~~ peel off —
Old
Dead hands, dead stringencies!
~~I am bare~~
I am white
Godiva

Rising, galloper,
In a season of dying,
A season of burning.

~~In a~~ season of burning, I
am White Godiva
On fire, my hair

My one resort
Brown furrows, rippling

White ~~Godiva I~~
Godiva, I unpeel —
Dead hands, dead stringencies!

White
Godiva, I unpeel —
Dead hands, dead stringencies!

Ariel

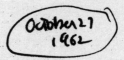October 27
1962

Stasis in darkness,
Then the substanceless blue
Pour of tor and distances.

God's lioness!
How one we grow!
Pivot of heels and knees! the furrow

Splits and passes,
Sister to the brown arc
Of the neck I cannot catch,

Nigger-eye
Berries cast dark
Hooks----

Black sweet blood mouthfuls!
Shadows!
Something else

Hauls me through air----
Thighs, hair;
Flakes from my heels.

White
Godiva, I unpeel----
Dead hands, dead stringencies!

And now I
Foam to wheat, a glitter of seas.
The child's cry

Melts in the wall.
O bright
Beast, I

Am the arrow, the dew that flies
Suicidal, at one with the drive
Into the red

Eye, the cauldron of morning.

October 27
1962   Sylvia Plath

Ariel

Stasis in darkness.
Then the substanceless blue
Pour of tor and distances.

God's lioness!
How one we grow!
Pivot of heels and knees! the furrow

Splits and passes,
Sister to the brown arc
Of the neck I cannot catch,

Nigger-eye
Berries cast dark
Hooks----

Black sweet blood mouthfuls!
Shadows!
Something else

Hauls me through air----
Thighs, hair;
Flakes from my heels.

White
Godiva, I unpeel----
Dead hands, dead stringencies!

And now I
Foam to wheat, a glitter of seas.
The child's cry

Melts in the wall.
O bright
And Beast, I

Am the arrow, The dew that flies
Suicidal, at one with the drive
Into the red

Eye, the cauldron of morning.

Ariel

Stasis in darkness.
Then the substanceless blue
Pour of tor and distances.

God's lioness!
How one we grow!
Pivot of heels and knees! the furrow

Splits and passes,
Sister to the brown arc
Of the neck I cannot catch,

Nigger-eye
Berries cast dark
Hooks----

Black sweet blood mouthfuls!
Shadows!
Something else

Hauls me through air---
Thighs, hair;
Flakes from my heels.

White
Godiva, I unpeel----
Dead hands, dead stringencies!

And now I
Foam to wheat, a glitter of seas.
The child's cry

Melts in the wall.
And I
Am the arrow,

The dew that flies
Suicidal, at one with the drive
Into the red

Eye, the cauldron of morning.

Ariel

Stasis in darkness.
Then the substanceless blue
Pour of tor and distances.

God's lioness!
How one we grow!
Pivot of heels and knees! the furrow

Splits and passes,
Sister to the brown arc
Of the neck I cannot catch,

Nigger-eye
Berries cast dark
Hooks---

Black sweet blood mouthfuls!
Shadows!
Something else

Hauls me through air---
Thighs, hair;
Flakes from my heels.

White
Godiva, I unpeel---
Dead hands, dead stringencies!

And now I
Foam to wheat, a glitter of seas.
The child's cry

Ariel (2)

Melts in the wall.
O bright
Beast, I

Am the arrow, the dew that flies
Suicidal, at one with the drive
Into the red

Eye, the cauldron of morning.

Sylvia Plath

Ariel

Stasis in darkness.
Then the substanceless blue
Pour of tor and distances.

God's lioness!
How one we grow!
Pivot of heels and knees! the furrow

Splits and passes, sister to
The brown arc
Of the neck I cannot catch,

Nigger-eye
Berries cast dark
Hooks———

Black sweet blood mouthfuls!
Shadows!
Somethingelse

Hauls me through air———
Thighs, hair;
Flakes from my heels.

White
Godiva, I unpeel———
Dead hands, dead stringencies!

And now I
Foam to wheat, a glitter of seas.
The child's cry

Melts in the wall.
And I
Am the arrow,

The dew that flies
Suicidal, at one with the drive
Into the red

Eye, the cauldron of morning.

Sylvia Plath

Ariel

Stasis in darkness.
Then the substanceless blue
Pour of tor and distances.

God's lioness!
How one we grow!
Pivot of heels and knees! the furrow

Splits and passes, sister to
The brown arc
Of the neck I cannot catch,

Nigger-eye
Berries cast dark
Hooks---

Black sweet blood mouthfuls!
Shadows!
Something else

Hauls me through air---
Thighs, hair;
Flakes from my heels.

White
Godiva, I unpeel---
Dead hands, dead stringencies!

And now I
Foam to wheat, a glitter of seas.
The child's cry

Melts in the wall.
And I
Am the arrow,

The dew that flies
Suicidal, at one with the drive
Into the red

Eye, the cauldron of morning.

PROOFS TO
SYLVIA PLATH,

ARIEL

Stasis in darkness.
Then the substanceless blue
Pour of tor and distances.

God's lioness,
How one we grow,
Pivot of heels and knees ! the furrow

Splits and passes, sister to
The brown arc
Of the neck I cannot catch,

Nigger-eye
Berries cast dark
Hooks—

Black sweet blood mouthfuls,
Shadows,
Something else

Hauls me through air—
Thighs, hair ;
Flakes from my heels.

White
Godiva, I unpeel—
Dead hands, dead stringencies

And now I
Foam to wheat, a glitter of seas.
The child's cry

Melts in the wall.
And I
Am the arrow,

The dew that flies
Suicidal, at one with the drive
Into the red

Eye, the cauldron of morning.

SYLVIA PLATH

Proofs to :—
SYLVIA PLATH

POPPIES IN OCTOBER — — — — —

Even the sun-clouds this morning cannot manage such skirts.
Nor the woman in the ambulance
Whose red heart blooms through her coat so astoundingly—

A gift, a love gift
Utterly unasked for
By a sky

Palely and flamily
Igniting its carbon monoxides, by eyes
Dulled to a halt under bowlers.

O my God, what am I
That these late mouths should cry open
In a forest of frost, in a dawn of cornflowers !
SYLVIA PLATH,

APPENDIX I
'The Swarm'

The bee poem 'The Swarm' appears on the contents page of the *Ariel and other poems* manuscript with parentheses around it in Sylvia Plath's own hand. She did not include the poem within the manuscript itself. Ted Hughes included it in the U.S. version of *Ariel* when it was first published in 1966. This restored edition maintains Sylvia Plath's editorial decision and does not include the poem in the main body of *Ariel and other poems*. The poem follows, along with a facsimile of a typescript draft.

The Swarm

Somebody is shooting at something in our town——
A dull pom, pom in the Sunday street.
Jealousy can open the blood,
It can make black roses.
What are they shooting at?

It is you the knives are out for
At Waterloo, Waterloo, Napoleon,
The hump of Elba on your short back,
And the snow, marshalling its brilliant cutlery
Mass after mass, saying Shh,

Shh. These are chess people you play with,
Still figures of ivory.
The mud squirms with throats,
Stepping stones for French bootsoles.
The gilt and pink domes of Russia melt and float off

In the furnace of greed. Clouds! Clouds!
So the swarm balls and deserts
Seventy feet up, in a black pine tree.
It must be shot down. Pom! Pom!
So dumb it thinks bullets are thunder.

It thinks they are the voice of God
Condoning the beak, the claw, the grin of the dog
Yellow-haunched, a pack dog,
Grinning over its bone of ivory
Like the pack, the pack, like everybody.

The bees have got so far. Seventy feet high.
Russia, Poland and Germany.

The mild hills, the same old magenta
Fields shrunk to a penny
Spun into a river, the river crossed.

The bees argue, in their black ball,
A flying hedgehog, all prickles.
The man with grey hands stands under the honeycomb
Of their dream, the hived station
Where trains, faithful to their steel arcs,

Leave and arrive, and there is no end to the country.
Pom, pom. They fall
Dismembered, to a tod of ivy.
So much for the chariots, the outriders, the Grand Army.
A red tatter, Napoleon.

The last badge of victory.
The swarm is knocked into a cocked straw hat.
Elba, Elba, bleb on the sea.
The white busts of marshals, admirals, generals
Worming themselves into niches.

How instructive this is!
The dumb, banded bodies
Walking the plank draped with Mother France's upholstery
Into a new mausoleum,
An ivory palace, a crotch pine.

The man with grey hands smiles——
The smile of a man of business, intensely practical.
They are not hands at all
But asbestos receptacles.
Pom, pom! 'They would have killed *me*.'

Stings big as drawing pins!
It seems bees have a notion of honor,
A black, intractable mind.
Napoleon is pleased, he is pleased with everything.
O Europe. O ton of honey.

4. The Swarm

Somebody is shooting at something in our town---
A dull pom, pom in the Sunday street.
Jealousy can open the blood,
It can make black roses.
What are they shooting at?

It is you the knives are out for
At Waterloo, Waterloo, Napoleon,
The hump of Elba on your short back,
And the snow, marshalling its brilliant cutlery
Mass after mass, saying Shh!

Shh! These are chess people you play with,
Still figures of ivory.
The mud squirms with throats,
Stepping stones for French bootsoles.
The gilt and pink domes of Russia melt and float off

In the furnace of greed. Clouds! Clouds!
So the swarm balls and deserts
Seventy feet up, in a black pine tree.
It must be shot down. Pom! Pom!
So dumb it thinks bullets are thunder.

It thinks they are the voice of God
Condoning the beak, the claw, the grin of the dog
Yellow-haunched, a pack dog,
Grinning over its bone of ivory
Like the pack, the pack, like everybody.

The bees have got so far. Seventy feet high!
Russia, Poland and Germany!
The mild hills, the same old magenta

Fields shrunk to a penny
Spun into a river, the river crossed.

The bees argue, in their black ball,
A flying hedgehog, all prickles.
The man with grey hands stands under the honeycomb
Of their dream, the hived station
Where trains, faithful to their steel arcs,

Leave and arrive, and there is no end to the country.
Pom, pom! They fall
Dismembered, to a tod of ivy.
So much for the chariots, the outriders, the Grand Army!
A red tatter, Napoleon!

The last badge of victory.
The swarm is knocked into a cocked straw hat.
Elba, Elba, bleb on the sea!
The white busts of marshals, admirals, generals
Worming themselves into niches.

How instructive this is!
The dumb, banded bodies
Walking the plank draped with Mother France's upholstery
Into a new mausoleum,
An ivory palace, a croth pine.

The man with grey hands smiles---
The smile of a man of business, intensely practical.
They are not hands at all
But asbestos receptacles.
Pom, pom! 'They would have killed me.'

Stings big as drawing pins!
It seems bees have a notion of honor,
A black, intractable mind.
Napoleon is pleased, he is pleased with everything.
O Europe! O ton of honey!

APPENDIX II
Script for the BBC broadcast 'New Poems by Sylvia Plath'

In a letter from December 14, 1962, later published in *Letters Home: Correspondence, 1950–1963*, Sylvia Plath wrote to her mother, Aurelia, that she 'spent last night writing a long broadcast of all my new poems to submit to an interested man at the BBC'. The man referred to at the British Broadcasting Corporation was Douglas Cleverdon. The script that follows includes notes for 'The Applicant', 'Lady Lazarus', 'Daddy', 'Sheep in Fog' (which was not included in Sylvia Plath's manuscript *Ariel and other poems*), 'Ariel', 'Death & Co.', 'Nick and the Candlestick', and 'Fever 103°.'

These new poems of mine have one thing in common. They were all written at about four in the morning—that still, blue, almost eternal hour before cockcrow, before the baby's cry, before the glassy music of the milkman, settling his bottles. If they have anything else in common, perhaps it is that they are written for the ear, not the eye: they are poems written out loud.

In this poem, called 'The Applicant', the speaker is an executive, a sort of exacting super-salesman. He wants to be sure the applicant for his marvelous product really needs it and will treat it right.

———

This poem is called 'Lady Lazarus'. The speaker is a woman who has the great and terrible gift of being reborn. The only trouble is, she has to die first. She is the phoenix, the libertarian spirit, what you will. She is also just a good, plain, very resourceful woman.

Here is a poem spoken by a girl with an Electra complex. Her father died while she thought he was God. Her case is complicated by the fact that her father was also a Nazi and her mother very possibly part Jewish. In the daughter the two strains marry and paralyze each other—she has to act out the awful little allegory once over before she is free of it.

In this next poem, the speaker's horse is proceeding at a slow, cold walk down a hill of macadam to the stable at the bottom. It is December. It is foggy. In the fog there are sheep.

Another horseback riding poem, this one called 'Ariel', after a horse I'm especially fond of.

This poem—'Death & Co.'—is about the double or schizophrenic nature of death—the marmoreal coldness of Blake's death mask, say, hand in glove with the fearful softness of worms, water and the other katabolists. I imagine these two aspects of death as two men, two business friends, who have come to call.

In this poem, 'Nick and the Candlestick', a mother nurses her baby son by candlelight and finds in him a beauty which, while it may not ward off the world's ill, does redeem her share of it.

This poem is about two kinds of fire—the fires of hell, which merely agonize, and the fires of heaven, which purify. During the poem, the first sort of fire suffers itself into the second. The poem is called 'Fever 103°'.

Notes

By David Semanki

SECTION I, *Ariel and other poems*

The printed poems follow the order of Sylvia Plath's manuscript *Ariel and other poems*. The definitive edition of each poem derives from Sylvia Plath's manuscript. All of the poems in the manuscript are present in *The Collected Poems,* edited by Ted Hughes.

Sylvia Plath in the manuscript uses three dots under punctuation that she wants to restore. All the dashes within the poems of this edition are now one standard length unlike in *The Collected Poems.* All the underlined words that appear in the manuscript have been changed to italics. Some poems contained within this volume differ from the version published in *The Collected Poems.* The poems, as previously published, may contain punctuation and spelling not dictated by the manuscript. We have here printed the poems in accordance with Sylvia Plath's manuscript.

Here follows a complete listing of Sylvia Plath's punctuation and word choices in contrast to the version printed in *The Collected Poems,* arranged thus: restored edition] *Collected Poems*

Morning Song 4 statue] statue. **8** distils] distills
The Couriers 10 Alps,] Alps. **12** grey] gray
Thalidomide 5 appal] appall
The Applicant 1 person] a person
A Secret 17 secret!] secret . . . **26** head!] head – **27** drawer.] drawer!
  33 Do] 'Do **40** stampede –] stampede! **41** twirling,] twirling
  gutterals.] gutturals!
The Jailor *title*: Jailor] Jailer **28** subversion] subversion, **45** me.] me!
Cut *dedication*: for] For

Elm *dedication*: for] For *the dedication has been placed in parentheses*

The Night Dances *an extra line-space reintroduced between stanzas 7 and 8,*
dividing the poem into equal halves of 14 lines each

The Detective **15** No-one] No one

Death & Co **1** Two. Of] Two, of

Lesbos **10** a schizophrenic] schizophrenic **11** panic.] panic, **26** you,]
you. **27** Mama] mama **39** t.b.] T.B. **41** Hollywood] in Hollywood
52 jewel.] jewel! valuable.] valuable! **63** They] He

The Other *an extra line-space reintroduced between stanzas 8 and 9, dividing the*
poem into equal halves of 16 lines each

Poppies in October *the dedication* for Helder and Suzette Macedo *has*
been restored **12** cornflowers!] cornflowers.

The Courage of Shutting-Up **3, 5, 16** discs] disks **5** heard,] heard –
20 going.] going! **21** by] by, **25** time!] time.

Nick and the Candlestick **2** stalacmites] stalactites

Berck-Plage **2** inflammation!] inflammation. **32** throat!] throat . . .
64 whitely,] whitely **73** grey] gray **91** unnatural] natural

Getting There **4** appal] appall **56** *an* is *placed between parentheses in Plaths's*
typescript

Medusa **13** you,] you **26** Paralyzing] Paralysing **31** X ray] X-ray

Purdah **8** valuable.] valuable! **19** arrives,] arrives **20** mirrors.]
mirrors! **25** curtain.] curtain **35** macaws.] macaws! **45** plies] flies
46 crystals,] crystals

The Moon and the Yew Tree **5** Fumey] Fumy

A Birthday Present **14** all,] all **39** cotton –] cotton. **50** cold,] cold

Letter in November **14** Wellingtons] wellingtons **28** grey] gray

Amnesiac **1** Recognize.] Recognize! **4** wife] wife – **6** cocker.] cooker!
15 barren.] barren! **18** rears,] rears **19** tail.] tail!

Daddy **9** grey] gray **27** *a period replaces a comma after the final* ich **38** gypsy]
gipsy **43** moustache] mustache **45** o You] O You **60** do] do.

Fever 103° **52** Nor] Not

The Bee Meeting **15** beanfield,] beanfield. **39** cow parsley]
cow-parsley

The Arrival of the Bee Box **17** appals] appalls

Stings **9** it.] it, **12** grey] gray

Wintering **16** *the 's' has been accidentally dropped from* Chinese *in Plaths's type-script; the correct spelling has always been used in the published poem*

SECTION II, Facsimile of the manuscript for *Ariel and other poems*

Sylvia Plath's manuscript *Ariel and other poems* consists of sheets of $8^{1}/_{2} \times 11$ inches cream-coloured typing paper. She used a black typewriter ribbon.

Sylvia Plath's name and Devon address appear in the upper right-hand corner on the original and carbon copy sheets of the two discarded title pages of the manuscript in the Smith College archive. On both sheets, Plath has used black pen. The original discarded title page reads 'Daddy'. 'A Birthday Present', 'The Rabbit Catcher', and 'The Rival' are deleted. On the discarded carbon copy title page of 'Daddy,' 'A Birthday Present' and 'The Rival' are deleted.

Plath created two identical dedication pages, again using carbon copy paper. Only the original is reproduced here.

She also created two identical contents pages by use of carbon copy paper. On the original contents page, all of Plath's marks are in black ink, except for the mark in red over the 'h' of 'Death & Co.'; the other mark in red is in the lower right hand of the page. On the carbon copy contents page, she underlined in red the titles of poems that were accepted for publication and typed or wrote the place of publication next to each title. All handwritten annotations are in black ink except for the word 'Poetry' opposite 'Purdah' and 'Fever 103°', which is written in red. It is possible that some of the annotations were made as late as January 25, 1963, when the *London Magazine* accepted a number of Plath's poems for its April 1963 issue.

On all the original working drafts of 'Ariel' where Sylvia Plath has typed her name in the upper right-hand corner, she has also included her Devon address. The original typeset proof of 'Ariel' from the *Observer* contains Sylvia Plath's Devon address in two places under her name.

APPENDIX I

The Swarm **5** What] Who **9** marshalling] marshaling **10** Shh,] Shh! **11** Shh.] Shh! **16** Clouds! Clouds!] Clouds, clouds. **23** pack dog] pack-dog **26** high.] high! **27** Germany.] Germany! **33** grey] gray **37** Pom, pom.] Pom! Pom! **39** chariots] charioteers Army.] Army! **40** Napoleon. Napoleon! **43** sea.] sea! **51** grey] gray **55** Pom, pom!] Pom! Pom! **58** black,] black **60** Europe.] Europe! honey.] honey!

The four previously published volumes of Sylvia Plath's poetry

Ariel [A] Faber & Faber, London, 1965; Harper & Row, NY, 1966

Crossing the Water [CW] Faber & Faber, London, 1971; Harper & Row, NY, 1971

Winter Trees [WT] Faber & Faber, London, 1971; Harper & Row, NY, 1972

The Collected Poems [CP] Faber & Faber, London, 1981; Harper & Row, NY, 1981

The following are the dates of composition for Sylvia Plath's poems in *Ariel and other poems* as established in *The Collected Poems* and on the manuscripts at Smith College. The bracketed abbreviations indicate the Sylvia Plath volume in which the poem first appeared.

'Morning Song' (19 February 1961) [A]
'The Couriers' (4 November 1962) [A]
'The Rabbit Catcher' (21 May 1962) [WT]
'Thalidomide' (4–8 November 1962) [WT]
'The Applicant' (11 October 1962) [A]
'Barren Woman' (21 February 1961) [CP]
'Lady Lazarus' (23–29 October 1962) [A]
'Tulips' (18 March 1961) [A]
'A Secret' (10 October 1962) [CP]
'The Jailor' (17 October 1962) [CP]
'Cut' (24 October 1962) [A]
'Elm' (12–19 April 1962) [A]
'The Night Dances' (4–6 November 1962) [A]
'The Detective' (1 October 1962) [WT]
'Ariel' (27 October 1962) [A]
'Death & Co.' (12–14 November 1962) [A]
'Magi' (1960) [CW]
'Lesbos' (18 October 1962) [A]
'The Other' (2 July 1962) [WT]
'Stopped Dead' (19 October 1962) [WT]
'Poppies in October' (27 October 1962) [A]
'The Courage of Shutting-Up' (2 October 1962) [WT]
'Nick and the Candlestick' (24 October 1962) [A]
'Berck-Plage' (28–30 June 1962) [A]
'Gulliver' (3–6 November 1962) [A]
'Getting There' (3–6 November 1962) [A]
'Medusa' (28 October 1962) [WT]
'Purdah' (28 October 1962) [WT]
'The Moon and the Yew Tree' (22 October 1961) [A]
'A Birthday Present' (30 September 1962) [A]
'Letter in November' (11 November 1962) [A]
'Amnesiac' (21 October 1962) [WT]
'The Rival' (July 1961) [A]
'Daddy' (12 October 1962) [A]
'You're' (January/February 1960) [A]

'Fever 103°' (20 October 1962) [A]
'The Bee Meeting' (3 October 1962) [A]
'The Arrival of the Bee Box' (4 October 1962) [A]
'Stings' (6 October 1962) [A]
'The Swarm' (7 October 1962) [A]
'Wintering' (8–9 October 1962) [A]

The following poems are listed in the order of the contents of the published volume of *Ariel*. Those with dates indicate poems that were not originally part of the manuscript *Ariel and other poems*. These dates refer to the dates of composition as established in *The Collected Poems* and on the manuscripts at Smith College.

'Morning Song'
'The Couriers'
'Sheep in Fog' (2 December 1962, 28 January 1963)
'The Applicant'
'Lady Lazarus'
'Tulips'
'Cut'
'Elm'
'The Night Dances'
'Poppies in October'
'Berck-Plage'
'Ariel'
'Death & Co.'
'Lesbos' (not included in original U.K. edition, but included in original U.S. edition)
'Nick and the Candlestick'
'Gulliver'
'Getting There'
'Medusa'
'The Moon and the Yew Tree'
'A Birthday Present'
'Mary's Song' (18–19 November 1962) (not included in original U.K.

edition, but included in original U.S. edition)

'Letter in November'

'The Rival'

'Daddy'

'You're'

'Fever 103°'

'The Bee Meeting'

'The Arrival of the Bee Box'

'Stings'

'The Swarm' (not included in original U.K. edition, but included in
original U.S. edition)

'Wintering'

'The Hanging Man' (27 June 1960)

'Little Fugue' (2 April 1962)

'Years' (16 November 1962)

'The Munich Mannequins' (28 January 1963)

'Totem' (28 January 1963)

'Paralytic' (29 January 1963)

'Balloons' (5 February 1963)

'Poppies in July' (20 July 1962)

'Kindness' (1 February 1963)

'Contusion' (4 February 1963)

'Edge' (5 February 1963)

'Words' (1 February 1963)